D1360630

# I'M NO HERO

# I'm No Hero

## Journeys
## of a
## Holocaust
## Survivor

# HENRY FRIEDMAN

Foreword by Michael Berenbaum

*A Samuel & Althea Stroum Book*

UNIVERSITY OF WASHINGTON PRESS

SEATTLE & LONDON

*To Sandra*

*To Robert*

*To Deborah*

*To Jeffrey*

*because you play a very important part in my life*

This book is published with the assistance of a grant from the
Stroum Book Fund, established through the generosity of
Samuel and Althea Stroum.

Library of Congress Cataloging-in-Publication Data
can be found at the back of this book.

# Contents

# *Foreword*

I READ SURVIVORS' LITERATURE OFTEN. I READ their stories because I feel close to survivors. I read their accounts because survivors make history come alive; they are history incarnate. I read survivors' memoirs because from each of the memoirs I learn something different, something more than I knew before.

It was from survivors that I first learned of the Holocaust. Yet it was not from what they said. When I was growing up in the United States in the 1950s, survivors seldom spoke of their experiences, at least not to Americans and certainly not to children. Survivors were spoken of; they were spoken about in whispers, in sighs, but they were seldom questioned directly, and most certainly not about their experiences during those dark years.

My first images of the Holocaust are vivid to me. I was born after the war, so they came to me not in movie newsreels but in school. As a child in the Yeshiva of Central Queens in New York, a Hebrew-speaking day school, I had teachers with fists but no fingers, teachers with tattoos on their arms. Words were spoken quietly in hushed voices, words that were never to be repeated, words that we did not understand, that we *could* not understand — concentration camps, murder and ghettos, death and children. But the Holocaust remained unspeakable; survivors did not speak.

They did not speak, perhaps because they could not speak. They were too close to the Event; the loss was too near to them. Years later, this childhood experience would make clear to me the biblical story of Lot, who, together with his wife, fled his home in Sodom as it was being destroyed. His wife looked back as she was running away, and she was turned into a pillar of salt — the salt of tears. Paralyzed by grief, she could not move on. Lot was left with his daughters, who thought they were the last survivors on earth; they were the last women and he the last man. His daughters plotted as to how to create a future. They gave their father wine to drink, they seduced him, and they gave birth to two great nations. After life's destruction, they re-created life. Looking back could come only later; they devoted all their energies to moving on.

More important, if we listen carefully to survivors' accounts, they did not speak because they understood that no one was ready to listen. In the countries where they found refuge, people were interested in the future, not the past. In Israel, the place of refuge for most survivors, state-building was the primary task. The Holocaust symbolized life in exile, and exile was the logical outcome of statelessness and powerlessness. The future alone beckoned. In the United States, when survivors first spoke of the past they were quickly and often politely informed that "that was then and this is now." Everyone who came from Europe was escaping a past, leaving it behind, whether it was the famine of the Irish, the poverty of the Italians, or the persecution of the Jews. America was forward-looking. We did not look back.

Or when they spoke, they were asked an unanswerable question: "Why did you survive when no one else did?" There could be only one truthful response to the question: luck. Every survivor knew someone wiser and stronger, someone more able, someone more worthy who, by accidental circumstance and the ruthless tenacity of the killers, was murdered. The question "Why did you survive?" was often heard as a reproach, as an accusation suggesting betrayal or compromise — sexual or moral. The true answer could come only later, as the character of a survivor's life and accomplishments gave meaning to the lucky accident of survival. Henry Friedman can now answer that question by the quality of the life he has led, which has transformed survival into witness, an act of witness to the past, an offering to our collective future. He can answer that question by what he has worked to build in Seattle — an institute of Holocaust education and remembrance — and by what he has contributed to the establishment of the United States Holocaust Memorial Museum. He can answer it by speaking of his children and their children, of the continuity of Jewish life, and of the re-creation of human community in the aftermath of destruction.

Professionally, I have been engaged in two great tasks to give voice to the unspoken words of my youth and to bring the silence of those survivors to the American people and the world. The first project was the creation of the United States Holocaust Memorial Museum in Washington, D.C. The second is the ongoing work of the Survivors of the Shoah Visual History Foundation, which in five years has recorded more than 50,200 testimonies in fifty-seven countries and in thirty-two languages. The Shoah Foundation, established by Steven Spielberg after the filming of *Schindler's List*, has compiled more than 116,000 hours of testimony. It has been my fate in life to help bring to the American people, in an American idiom, what could not be told to me and to those of my generation by the Holocaust survivors, at least not then.

Their experience has now gone beyond the confines of the Jewish community. It is an offering that has transformed American values and shaped American policy in such a way that the president of the United States in 1999 — with his country's support — could intervene in Kosovo against "ethnic cleansing."

Henry Friedman's *I'm No Hero: Journeys of a Holocaust Survivor* is a slim but powerful volume. It traces one man's experiences from his comfortable childhood before the war into a life in hiding, together with his family and alone, through his postwar adventures as he rebuilds his life and re-creates a world. During the Nazi occupation Henry's father, Jacob Friedman, despite dwindling affluence and an ever-narrowing circle of contacts, is able to arrange secret shelter for his family. Because young Henry's Holocaust years are spent primarily in hiding and provide only rare glimpses of the larger shape of "The Final Solution to the Jewish Problem," his universe is small. But through the particular, the larger story emerges. Thus, only in passing do we learn of the ghettoization of the Jews and their struggles within the ghetto. We learn of deportation only through the absence of Jews. And Henry does not know of life inside the concentration camps.

Henry's family was saved because two women were willing to risk it all. Marie Symchuck confronted her husband, whose courage waned as the killings intensified and the consequence of hiding Jews—a death sentence—became ever more vivid. Mrs. Symchuck was not righteous in a conventional sense; throughout the occupation she carried on an affair in her own bed with the local police chief, a Nazi who wondered aloud as to the Friedmans' whereabouts. Her gossip with the chief, heard through the wall by the eavesdropping Henry, was a source of vital information for the Friedman family—and of fantasies and fascination for the adolescent boy. Marie Bazalchik, who hid Jacob Friedman alone, could not even tell her own family. She was decent; they were rabid anti-Semites. These two women endured mortal danger for themselves and their families because, unlike so many of their countrymen, they were appalled at what was being done to the Jews.

Lawrence Langer, the distinguished critic of Holocaust literature, or perhaps more accurately, the distinguished scholar of the Holocaust who uses literature as his lens of interpretation, has introduced the concept of *choiceless choices* into our understanding of the victim's plight. A choiceless choice is not between good and bad, or life and death, or even between the lesser of two evils. It is between "one form of abnormal response and another, both imposed by a situation that [is] not of the victim's own choosing." Friedman's narration of the fate of his infant sister, born in hiding, vividly illustrates this. As you read his words, think of the ordinary categories of right and wrong, the ordinary notions of choice. The circumstances of the Friedmans—and of so many victims of the Holocaust—will become clearer to you.

Friedman devotes many pages, even more pages than he devotes to the Holocaust story, to his postwar exploits—financial and sexual. These depictions may offend, but in truth they reveal much about his response to freedom after confinement. Once set free, the youthful Henry places no restraints on his life, neither the laws of the land nor the conventions of common morality. He demonstrates a zest for life, a celebration of life, a passion for life and its pleasures that seeks to compensate for what he has lost and can never recover. We must be grateful for his candor, which is revealed in detail after detail. He is in no mood for reflection during these chapters, yet the speed with which he sets aside the bon vivant's life after he meets and marries Sandy indicates that at some very deep level it had been unsatisfying. We are told of the birth of his children and of his growing financial success. From so diffuse and diverse a range of experiences, we witness the growth of seriousness and depth, the creation of family, the assumption of communal responsibility, a fidelity to remembering the past, and a commitment to the future. These qualities form the substance of a life that is satisfying and giving. They are the substance of a survivor's life.

MICHAEL BERENBAUM
*President, Survivors of the Shoah Visual History Foundation*
*Former Director of the Research Institute,*
*The United States Holocaust Memorial Museum*
*Professor of Theology, The University of Judaism*

# Acknowledgments

MY WIFE SANDRA IS VERY SPECIAL IN MANY ways. She spent months typing up my thoughts for this book after listening to hours and hours of tapes and unscrambling my handwritten notes. Without her help, this book would never have been written.

I would like to thank my youngest son, Jeffrey, who was ten years old when he first urged his brother and sister to buy me a tape recorder and suggested that I record my experiences from World War II. He knew how difficult it was for me to share the darkest years of my life because I was afraid that I would pass my pain on to my children. It was his vision and encouragement that got me started. I would also like to thank my first-born son, Robert, who kept asking me when I would finish my book. My daughter Deborah deserves my loving gratitude because she transcribed and printed all my tapes so I could read them. Reading through the many pages she printed for me was a valuable experience and brought additional information to my memory.

I am grateful to Steve Cutler, Lane Morgan, and Dr. Steve Schneider for their help in editing and improving my manuscript.

At the University of Washington Press, I especially thank Naomi Pascal, associate director and editor in chief, for not giving up on me and for encouraging me to do more work on my story. I am also very grateful to Julidta Tarver, managing editor.

Finally, I wish to express my deep appreciation to Sam Stroum, an outstanding community leader and a wonderful human being, for suggesting to me at the outset that I publish my story.

# SURVIVAL

# My
# Boyhood
# in Brody,
# Poland

I AM IN MY DEN WATCHING A VIDEO PRODUCED by my daughter. On the television screen are talking heads. A man explains how he ran into the forest and lived there like an animal for two years. A deaf woman contorts her face violently and gestures to describe her captors and her escape. An old couple with white hair talk about their time in hiding, how hungry they had been. All their faces look tired, yet their eyes say they are happy to be alive.

Outside, tall evergreens surround my house on Mercer Island, near Seattle. Lake Washington, with its sailboats and beaches, is only a stone's throw away. How far this is from my birthplace in Brody, Poland. What impossibly different worlds!

Soon, I too come up on the screen. Yes, that's me. My face is tanned, and I am wearing a gold neck chain with the golden letter *chai* ("life"). I begin to talk of that other world. Of my mother. Of my father. Of my aunts and uncles.

I REMEMBER PROUDLY carrying my father's prayer shawl in his blue bag with its embroidered Star of David to the Great Synagogue in Brody on Saturdays.

*German-Soviet Partition of Poland, September 1939*

I used to sit beside him on a wooden bench near the reading table at the front of the synagogue. The candles burned all through the service. You could smell the tallow in the air, mixed with perspiration and the stale breath of the worshipers. On Yom Kippur, father sat in synagogue the entire day. I longed for fresh air and counted the pages in the prayer book until *Yizkor*, the memorial service for the dead. When father stood, I rushed outside with the other children.

JEWS SETTLED IN BRODY IN 1588. Over time, the Jewish community established itself and thrived, a vigorous mix of scholars, professionals, merchants, and artisans. By the middle of the eighteenth century, trade in Brody was concentrated in Jewish hands. For many years Jews constituted a majority of the town's population, and at the outbreak of World War II, nearly 10,000 Jews lived in Brody itself, with some 5,000 more in the surrounding rural area.

The town of Brody lies in the West Ukraine region, which was part of Poland at the time of my birth in 1928. The region came under Soviet occupation following the partition of Poland in 1939, and Brody fell to the Germans in July 1941. Persecution and murder of the Jews began immediately thereafter. Between September and November 1942, in two *aktions*, a total of 4,500 Jews were sent to the Belzek death camp, and a ghetto was established in December 1942 for the 6,500 remaining Jews of Brody. By the end of 1942, young Jews formed a fighting unit in the ghetto which maintained contacts with partisans in the surrounding forest and with the non-Jewish resistance. From May to June, 1943, the Brody ghetto and labor camp were liquidated and the surviving 2,500 Jews were deported to the death camp at Majdanek. By all reports, no Jewish community has existed in Brody since World War II.*

We had a very old *shul*, or synagogue, which took up an entire city block. Several little shuls surrounded the Great Synagogue, and in them, tailors, shoemakers, and butchers could pray in small groups with fellow tradesmen.

Each small group was under the jurisdiction of Brody's chief rabbi. He was the law of the land. If there was a dispute over property, he would

---

*See *Encyclopedia of the Holocaust*, New York: Macmillan, 1990; Archives of the Nahum Goldmann Museum of the Jewish Diaspora.

preside over the Rabbinical Court's decision. If a man wanted to divorce his wife, he would need to petition the chief rabbi. If a young fellow wanted to get married, he would request the chief rabbi's signature. Even the Polish officers would salute the chief rabbi of Brody.

As a child, however, I was ruled by my mother and father. Mother, who kept a strictly kosher home, permitted us to eat non-kosher food outside our home and at restaurants.

"Just don't tell your father," she said.

My mother came from a family of lawyers and professionals. She, too, was well educated. She was very pretty and loved to dance at weddings. Father came from a family of farmers and merchants. He worked very hard, rising by five o'clock each morning to start his day. He admired mother, though they had the usual lively disagreements on small issues.

I remember once when I was seven or eight, I petitioned father to let me wear long side-locks, the type worn by Hasidic boys at the religious school I attended each afternoon.

"You don't have any rabbis in your family," he said. "You're not going to be the first one."

"But my friends all have side-locks," I said.

"I'm sorry," he said. "You're not going to change my mind. My sons will dress in suits, not black robes. Your hair will be cut at the ears."

We lived in a house attached to our busy textile store, which sold fabrics imported from as far away as London. Uncle Salomon, my father's youngest brother, lived in a neighboring village on a large farm that had once belonged to my paternal grandfather. My grandmother Klara lived with Salomon, his wife, Fanny, and their daughter, Sara. On the same parcel of land, in a house of their own, lived my father's sister, Aunt Freda, and her husband, Abraham, their son, Anschul, and their daughters, Pepe and Yite. The two families shared the barns and the equipment, but each maintained separate animals and managed separate finances. Grandma Klara kept peace between the two families, ruling with a strong hand and a strong sense of religion. She had been one of eleven children, and some of her brothers and sisters were poor, so she helped them out with food.

Uncle Joseph, the second of my father's brothers, also lived on a farm in the country with his wife, Lea, and their son, Mendel. Each of the three brothers lived in a separate district, about twenty-five kilometers (or just over fifteen miles) distant from one another, but close enough to share many good times. In 1942 we lost contact with my uncle Joseph and his family and never found them again.

THE FIRST WEDDING I attended was that of my uncle Salomon, who was the youngest child in my father's family. There was a great deal of excitement because the wedding was going to take place in Busk, which was about forty kilometers from Brody. Back then that was a long trip, and a decision had to be made whether we would travel by horse or take the train. We finally decided to go by train because the weather was not very nice at that time of the year. This would be my first train ride, and for two weeks all I could think of was meeting some of my cousins for the first time, and the wedding.

Most of my cousins at the wedding were older than I, and they liked me but they also got me in trouble. At their urging, another cousin and I crawled under the table and stole the shoes of some of the women; when the ladies wanted them back, my cousins made them pay ransom. This was very wrong, but, on the whole, we had a good time at the wedding. On our way home, however, my father wanted to know if I had had any part in the shoe-stealing scam, and I admitted that I had, not without a bit of pride. My mother instantly demanded that I be punished, while my father had to restrain himself from smiling. My mother came out on top by saying that I would never be allowed to attend another wedding, and I would receive more punishment when we got home. But my parents never did punish me — either they forgot, or decided to let me off this time.

I WAS SENT TO *cheder* (religious school) when I was four because my grandmother Klara became very upset with my father. He was raising a non-Jew, she said. When I visited Grandma, I could not speak any Yiddish because my nanny spoke to me only in Polish. The *cheder* was near the Great Synagogue. Its entrance had huge doors, and inside it was very dark, with just one light bulb. When I was seven, I went to public school during the day and *cheder* after school. This was until 1939. During the Soviet occupation, my brother and I had private tutoring in Jewish religion. A teacher would come all the way from Brody on a bicycle to our farm.

I attended public school with children from all over the city. I can't remember the day, or even the year, when I first heard my classmates mention Hitler. Perhaps it was 1937 or 1938. I had been playing soccer outside with my Jewish friends, while our non-Jewish schoolmates took a religious class.

We didn't mind. After all, we would go to *cheder* after school and study the Talmud. Besides, our absence gave us an excuse to play ball. Usually our Christian classmates joined us for a few minutes after their class. Recently one of them had kicked our soccer ball over the fence.

"Christ killer!" he said. "Wait until Hitler comes. He'll take care of you."

"Goy!" I shouted back.

"Kike!" he spat.

I reached out to hit him. My friend held me back.

"Come on," he said. "Forget about it."

WE COULDN'T FORGET about it, though. "Wait until Hitler comes" became a daily refrain in our schoolyard. I listened to stories about Hitler at home. My parents talked in the living room at night, and I could hear their voices from my bedroom. They spoke of leaving for Canada.

Grandmother, however, didn't want to leave her brothers and other relatives behind. She had no desire to start a new life in a different world. My aunt Freda was afraid to leave because her husband was not healthy. To start over in a foreign country with a sick husband and three children would not be easy. Uncle Salomon sided with grandmother. They would argue their point by saying "Look at Markus Pieniaker, how well he is doing in Germany!" Uncle Markus was my mother's brother who had come to visit us from Berlin in 1938, arriving in a chauffeur-driven car and looking wonderful. I remember a white handkerchief sticking out of his suit pocket like a three-pointed crown. "If Markus lived in Brody, he would be riding a horse, not a fancy car," they said. "So Hitler can't be all that bad to the Jews. The newspaper stories are just to frighten us, to fool us into leaving Poland and selling our property cheap to the goyim [non-Jews]."

"Salomon keeps dragging his feet," my father told my mother. "We're missing a good opportunity." What he had heard about the Nazis, he knew to be true, and he feared for our future. Still, like many families, ours made a decision collectively. Whenever it came to a vote, Salomon sided with Grandma and his sister Freda, leaving the two older brothers in the minority. After two years of arguments, Father and Joseph convinced the family to leave, but the war came to Poland sooner than anyone expected. Although our papers were almost ready, the borders were closed.

MY WISH WAS TO BE an officer in the cavalry unit of the Polish army when I grew up. I used to watch the army parade through my city, and I would visualize myself leading the whole cavalry. I even had the color of my horse picked out — it had to be black. But if I could not become a cavalry officer, my second choice was to become a lawyer because some of my uncles were lawyers. Unfortunately, as I was to learn, the Polish cavalry was no match for the German tanks.

The start of the war on September 22, 1939, was frightening. I was eleven years old. The first bombing began on a Friday night, the *Shabbes*. We spent that night in our coal cellar beneath the house. It was an eerie space, with candles flickering on the shelves. The earth shook with each explosion. All that night we shuddered through the storming of the town. We prayed more than once that we would not be buried alive. Father had counted the hours to dawn, when the bombing would stop, and at the first possible moment he rose to go upstairs.

He looked out on a desolate city, debris strewn everywhere. He came immediately downstairs to tell us we would be leaving.

"But it's *Shabbes*," Mother said.

"So what," my father retorted. "Our lives are at stake. The Germans will pound away again tonight."

"Where will we go?" she asked.

"To the farm," he replied. "They won't attack the countryside."

When I came out of our basement, what my eyes saw was a shock that I remember to this day — buildings burning, parts of human bodies, dead and wounded animals. I was mesmerized by a wounded horse. His blood was bubbling from his stomach, and my mother put her hand over my eyes and dragged me away. I must have seen more than my parents thought I saw, because as I merely write these words I find myself shaking, wet with perspiration.

THAT MORNING, ON OUR horse-and-buggy ride to the country-side, I saw hordes of people running toward the Romanian border. The roads were jammed with cars, trucks, buses, horses, cows, and people. Many carried with them their most prized possessions in a desperate dash for the south.

War, for those first days, seemed like a game to my brother and me. The planes dogfighting overhead provided us with amusement, and we would pick and choose the winners. In reality, the Polish army was doomed to defeat. Its planes were inferior. But all this was unknown to me as a child of eleven. I felt safe on my father's farm, in Suchowola, protected from the carnage around us.

The bombing lasted only two or three days. When it stopped, we could hardly believe it.

"Where are the Germans?" Mother asked.

"They'll be back," said Father.

But for now, all was silent. News came shortly that the Russians would occupy Brody. Hitler had signed a pact with Stalin, ceding Brody and the rest of the Ukraine to the Russians.

We were relieved, except for Father. He hated the Russians. He had seen them cross the border into Poland during World War I. He remembered their beating of Jews, their robbing and raping of women. He had lived near the Russian border in a small village that was then a part of the Austro-Hungarian Empire.

THE RUSSIANS NOW CAME on foot, in tanks, and on horses. One of the first acts of the occupying forces was to seize our family's textile store in town. "It's to be a collective," the lieutenant told my father.

"But we've worked for years to build this store," Father said. "It's our family business."

"It's to be a state-run store," the lieutenant told him.

My parents were given twenty-four hours to clear out. Our house in Brody, including most of our possessions, was also seized by the Russians. Unlike many of our friends who lost their businesses to communism, we at least had someplace else to go. The farm in Suchowola, always a summer retreat for us until now, became our permanent residence.

In Suchowola I attended a Russian school, which I enjoyed much more than the Polish school in Brody. I was no longer just another Jewish kid. In the Russian school you would be punished for slandering a Jew, or a Pole, or a Ukrainian for that matter. As a Jewish child under the Russians, if you minded your own business, you would be treated no differently from others. All religious classes were cut from the curriculum.

In 1941 I earned the title of *Otlichnik* (The Best). When I brought home my special diploma with a picture of Lenin on it, I handed it to Father proudly.

"You're not to display this diploma at home," he said. He hated Lenin as much as he did Hitler.

"But I have been honored," I said.

"No, you haven't."

He threw the diploma on the ground.

During the Russian occupation, my family still observed religious tradition. My mother would light the Friday night candles, but we would say our prayers at home because it was too far to walk from Suchowola to Brody. By custom, religious Jews walked to the synagogue. The day before a Jewish Holiday, my father drove us in the horse and buggy to Brody, where we would stay with relatives and could then walk to the synagogue. After the German occupation, we stopped going to the Brody synagogue even on High Holy Days. My mother nonetheless made sure to have the Friday night candles lit, and we would pray at home — only on a very few occasions did we miss our regular prayers.

THE RUSSIANS RAISED the taxes on our farm. Father, through sheer force of will, refused to cooperate.

"Kulak," the Russians called him. "Exploiter!"

He was the second largest landowner in Suchowola County, and the neighbors looked up to him. If Father relinquished his land to the Russians for a commune, the neighbors would have to do the same. Despite pressure, he refused to sign papers to release the farm. In another year or two, the communists would have acted by force, sending him and the rest of us to Siberian labor camps. For the time being, however, he refused to capitulate.

In the winter of 1940, many Jewish citizens of Brody, as well as Jewish refugees who had fled the German sector of occupied Poland, were forced onto trains that took them away to the Siberian camps. Prominent Jews from our community were taken. Each family, ours included, feared it would be in the next train load. The situation was deteriorating quickly. Uncle Salomon was drafted into the Soviet army, a ploy by which the communists could seize an absent owner's property to form a commune.

IN JUNE 1941, ON A Saturday night, bombs exploding in Brody awakened us from our sleep—we could see the city all ablaze. Father went outside and asked a Russian officer what was happening.

"It's just maneuvers," the Russian said. The city was burning, however. The Russians didn't know what had hit them.

In the morning we could see dogfights. Russian planes were shot down by the dozens. My heart raced with excitement, partially from the crash of war, partially from being in the midst of so much fear.

Germany again was at war, this time with the Soviet Union.

When the Germans finally moved in, it put a chill in my bones. With the stomping of their goose-stepping black boots and the clatter of their armor, they were very different from the bedraggled array of Russians who had previously occupied Brody. From miles away you could hear the approach of the Germans. Their thunder rippled through the earth.

We were plunged into gloom and fear. It took the Germans less than two weeks to reach Brody after that first Saturday-night bombing.

FATHER PREPARED FOR the worst. He began hiding most of our remaining possessions — clothing, furs, silverware, dishes, and shoes. Nearly everything we still owned was buried underground in the safekeeping of some trusted Ukrainian families. He no longer cared what happened to his store, having given up that dream months before. He was only concerned that the Germans would come and loot the farm.

One of the first acts of the Germans was to register all the local intelligentsia, both Jews and non-Jews. Doctors, lawyers, teachers, and accountants were told to register, each profession in a different section of town. Some could foresee what was happening and refused. After registration, the non-Jews were released. The Jews, however, were taken away, never to be heard from again. Jewish doctors were the one exception — they were needed in the town to attend to both Jews and non-Jews. Only recently did I read in an encyclopedia that 250 of the Jewish intellectuals in Brody were executed in cold blood following their "job registration." My family lost three relatives to this purge.

THE GERMANS TURNED many of the Ukrainians into policemen by promising them a free and independent state in exchange for their help. I had been wary of the Ukrainians ever since some of them had tried to set fire to my father's farm a couple of years before.

The toughest Jews in Brody were the horse dealers, called *koniers*. As a kid I was terrified of them. They traded horses, buying and reselling them to farmers. We used to call them horse thieves, because they would threaten those who didn't cooperate. Often a farmer would be forced to sell his horse for much less than its worth, only to discover the horse dealer had turned around and resold it for a much higher price. If you tried to question the *koniers'* business practices, they would threaten you with the crack of the whip. As a boy, it seemed to me that one of them could beat up ten others.

Although many Jews looked down on Jewish shoemakers and tailors, everyone feared the Jewish horse dealers. The Ukrainians could now prove themselves to the Germans by taking care of these bullies.

On the third day of the German occupation, the Ukrainian police rounded up the *koniers* and told them they were going to bury Russian soldiers and horses. It had become almost commonplace to see the dead and wounded strewn on the streets of Brody and all over the countryside. Today, it makes my stomach turn to think of it. But at that time walking the streets and seeing what was going on, no matter how barbarous, had become almost a normal part of my daily life in Brody.

Many of the Red Army soldiers killed were at first taken prisoner by the Germans, who then marched these Russians through the town. The Germans were riding motorcycles or horses, while the Russians, on aching feet, were tired and thirsty. If one fell and could not go on, he was promptly shot. If one reached out for water, the Germans would beat him as well as the person who tried to help him. These were the first acts of German brutality I witnessed.

The Ukrainians ordered the *koniers* to dig mass graves for the Russian dead in the woods at the edge of town. The bodies had been piled there and needed to be buried.

The horse dealers worked assiduously to dig the trenches, a job that took them several hours. Several of the Ukrainian policemen hid behind trees with their machine guns. A group of German enforcers, the *Einsatzgruppen,* now gave them their instructions. After the trenches were dug, the Ukrainians opened fire. The Polish Jews, shot in the back, fell into the trenches they had dug for the Russians. A few who were wounded managed to drag themselves out that night and lived to tell us the story.

The Germans immediately established a Jewish Council in Brody, the *Judenrat*, and an unarmed Jewish police force, the *Ordnungsdienst* (O.D.'s).

During the second week of the German occupation, while my father was away at his chores, a captain with two soldiers drove out to our farmhouse in a big truck. His men took everything except for a few pieces of furniture. Just as the captain hopped aboard the truck to leave, he looked back at us huddling in front of the house. He glared at the wedding ring on my mother's finger and came running toward her. She fled into the house. I was thirteen at the time, and I ran after my mother. The German grabbed her, trying to yank the ring off her finger. She was screaming. I pushed the captain away, but he slapped my face so hard I fell to the floor. I got up and ran to the clothes closet, where I knew my father had stored a gun. I jumped up on the bed, which was near the closet, to look on the shelf.

I wanted to kill this brute. But the gun wasn't there. Later, I found out my father had hidden the gun immediately before the Russians first occupied Brody. I went over to my mother. She was sobbing. The skin on her finger was chafed; the ring was missing.

"Heniek," she said, "you shouldn't have done that. We could have all been killed."

"I want to kill him."

She looked at me, afraid.

HANS FRANK, THE Nazi governor for our area, issued the order that all Jews over the age of six had to wear an armband with the six-point star on it. One time my mother and a cousin of mine went to a part of the city where they were afraid of being tormented because they were Jews, so they hid their armbands. Ukrainian police, however, were able to identify them as Jews. My mother was beaten on her upper arms so badly that she could not lift them for a month. My cousin, who was fourteen years old, was made to empty the waste from an outhouse with only her hands. Afterwards, she threw up for weeks, unable to eat. This was a minor punishment, though, considering that others had been killed for the same infraction. No one seemed willing to protect Jews at that time. Instead, all seemed willing to rape, rob, and murder them.

Later, when my own children were small, at times I had to change their diapers. While doing so, I would sometimes choke and hold myself from throwing up, not because of my own children, but because it would bring back thoughts of my cousin and the hours it took her to empty that outhouse of human waste.

AFTER THE GERMAN occupation, Jewish children were forbidden to go to school and Jewish teachers were forbidden to teach. My father was concerned that my brother and I would lose our chance for education, as he himself had done in World War I. He had finished only three grades of grammar school. My parents knew a young Jewish teacher who lived alone in Brody. From the very first day of the German occupation, she came to live with us on the farm. My father had offered her room and board on the farm if she would keep up our education and also help out with some farm chores.

Her name was Sarah. She came from an upper-class intellectual family. She dressed plainly, in a simple black dress. Sarah carried a Russian passport and read Marx. She had originally come to Brody from Bialystok to teach at our school. She was very strict with us. Over time we came to view her as another member of the family.

The Germans very quickly took over our farm. The farm was now run by Herr Johann Wolfgang, a half-German, half-Polish overseer from Silesia (the eastern part of Germany) appointed by the Germans. We became laborers with no authority on our own farm, plowing, planting, and maintaining the barns according to our daily assignments. We received no money. In fact, we had to pay the overseer so that we could continue to work and have food to eat. Still, we were very glad to be away from Brody.

One morning just at dawn, in February 1942, an eighteen-year-old girl who worked as a maid in the police station ran out to the house to awaken us. Her name was Julia Symchuck.

"Mr. Jacob!" she yelled from outside my father's window. "Get up! The Gestapo are coming after you. Please run. Run! Otherwise they will take you away!"

My parents quickly got us out of bed. We dressed in a hurry. Father ran out the back door. I ran after him to warn my mother's brother, Uncle Moshe, who lived next door. When I got back to the house, the Germans were searching all the rooms, looking for my father.

"Where is he?" they demanded.

"He's already gone to the fields," my mother said. "He's left."

They marched out of the house to search the barns. Father had picked out a niche in the attic of the horse barn for such an occasion. One of the Germans walked toward this barn, went inside, and decided to climb the rickety ladder up to the attic, where hay was stored. He hit his head on the roof.

"Shit!" he said. "If I catch that bastard up here, I'll throw him down." He inched closer toward Father. Had he reached out, he probably would have touched him. But for some reason he looked away and climbed back down the ladder.

Father spent the next three weeks in hiding. We were prisoners now. Our movement was prohibited without passes. If Herr Wolfgang had not considered us valuable in helping him run the farm, I'm sure he would have turned us over to the Gestapo in Brody.

As the days passed, Mother decided she would go to Mr. Kostek, the chief of police, a Ukrainian, to talk to him about Father.

"What will it take to save him?" she asked.

"You know."

It so happened that, because of our preparations to leave Poland for Canada, my father had started to accumulate U.S. dollars in the years 1938–39. I don't know what would have happened to us without those U.S. dollars.

My mother paid the chief of police $3,000, a fortune in those days, in that part of the country. That afternoon Father returned from hiding, frail and shaken.

We heard more rumors about the labor camps. We heard that people were dying from hunger, from being worked to death. At one time, we thought these stories exaggerated. No one ever returned to tell us what really happened. We had seen how these Nazis operated. They were mean, violent, hostile. Little did we know their capacity for evil. The word "demonic" had not yet crossed our lips.

We got wind in advance of the second roundup, or *aktion*. The

Germans again would take their quota — 3,000 Jews. This time all five of us went into hiding. I hid in the hayloft of one of the barns in the nearby fields belonging to the Polish prince whose castle was about forty-five kilometers from Suchowola.

I remember curling up in the hay for what seemed like weeks. At one point a field hand came in to bale some hay. The pitchfork pierced my arm. Don't scream, I told myself. Don't. Somehow, I managed not to. I was cut, but I didn't say a word.

No food for two days and a night and no water to drink because Father had told me not to leave this place. I was hungry. During the second night I sneaked out for some water and discovered six fresh eggs. I sucked them quickly, all six of them, and I ate some small sugar beets. Then I crept back to my fetal position, curled up in the hay. When Father came to tell me it was safe, I didn't know whether I was asleep or dreaming. At first I didn't move.

"Get up, Hersh," Father said in Yiddish. "Get up." (Hersh was my Yiddish nickname.)

When the hunt for Jews was over, we went back and found our house completely ransacked. The front door was smashed in. We felt devastated and empty at the destruction. But the next day, when we learned that many of our relatives had been taken away to camps, we knew what real loss was. They had not believed my father's urgent warnings. My mother wept and wept for her brother, Moshe Pieniaker. My father kept up a brave front. He knew the danger we were still facing, but he wore his confident air to keep us strong.

This time we had been lucky, but what about the next? As our farm was ten kilometers from the city, thus far we had not been exposed to the daily brutality of the Nazis. Working in the fields each day, I had time to think. What kind of future would I have living in fear, in a world where even my non-Jewish erstwhile friends hated me because I was Jewish? These were the same friends to whom I had given food when they were hungry before the war. I had a difficult time understanding why the Christian people hated me — a fourteen-year-old boy who was being forced to work and act like an adult under the Nazi reign. It was hard for me to live this kind of life — from day one of my entering the world up to the start of the war in 1939, I had been pampered very much as a baby and a child. I had also been a very finicky eater and my mother used to bribe me with money, or she would chase after me with a bowl of food so I would take at least a spoonful of mashed carrots, because it was "good for me."

During the second *aktion*, Jew had turned against Jew. These were the O.D.'s, Jewish police who actually helped the Germans find and arrest their own people. The O.D.'s wore blue uniforms and carried sticks. Their uniforms were purchased with money assessed like a tax from their fellow Jews. They ingratiated themselves with the Germans by helping to maintain civil order. I remember how much I hated these "traitors," as I called them.

The O.D.'s got theirs, though. During the second *aktion* they were told to bring their close relatives into the administration buildings for protection. When they were gathered into one place, it was easy for the Germans to persuade them all to board trucks that would transport them to a new "safe" location. Those of us left behind were not unhappy when we heard they were taken to the same camps as their brethren. The entire Jewish Council (Judenrat), including the mayor and the town's Jewish administrators, were taken away during the second *aktion*.

A silence settled over the city. Rumors about the camps swirled around us like bits of scrap from a windstorm. Even my father, who had never trusted the Russians or Germans, didn't believe things were as horrible as we were hearing. To this day I don't know why we didn't fathom the darkness of the German plan. Why couldn't we have communicated their intentions? But to whom? The community was left leaderless.

In the midst of these rumors, I remember hearing of the *shammes's* dream. The *shammes* was a pious older man who watched the synagogue, was there three times a day for services, and saw that there was the necessary quorum for prayer. Now the synagogue was quiet. The rabbis who prayed for the Messiah either had been deported or were staying away. In the *shammes's* dream, two candles were buried on a windowsill in the synagogue along the eastern wall that faced Jerusalem. A voice told him to remove a few bricks from the wall and to light the two candles. By the time the candles burned all the way down, God would have found a way to kill Hitler.

Word of the *shammes's* dream spread. To help God fulfill the dream, the remaining Jews of Brody lit candles at an appointed time, praying for the dream's predicted outcome as the candles melted.

Nothing happened.

ON A SPRING DAY IN 1942, after a day of work on the farm, Herr Wolfgang, the Silesian overseer, informed us that an order had been given for all the remaining Jews in the area to leave their homes and move into town, to live in a section of Brody now set up as a ghetto. This was being done "for security reasons."

That night we had a family meeting. "Once they have us behind barbed wire," my father said, "that will be the end of us. We cannot go. We must prepare."

"I will talk to the Silesian," he said. "He still needs us to run the farm. Meanwhile, as long as we can stay here, we must prepare for eventually going into hiding. The time will come when we must hide out for a long time. Who knows how long? Perhaps six months, perhaps more. We will not be allowed to return to our home."

The Silesian, under pressure to produce a big harvest, knew nothing about rotation farming. He depended upon Father and managed somehow to keep us out of the ghetto. We felt fortunate. Father used the time to prepare our hiding places. He had tried to help my uncle and our cousins, but he realized that he had to devote all his energy to saving us. We could associate with no one, not even former friends. It would have been dangerous to let anyone know where we were or what we were doing. We were in hiding before we ever disappeared.

By the middle of 1942, we had lost contact with everyone on my father's side of the family and with those on my mother's side who lived around Brody. People were gone, taken away, and no one saw them again. I don't remember seeing a smiling Jewish face in 1942.

One afternoon in October 1942, my father and I returned from the fields. The Silesian was waiting outside our house to talk with Father. They walked toward the barn together. I waited by our front door. Father's face told me something bad had happened.

"We have to go to the ghetto," he said.

"All right," I said. I knew we had other plans. We would only appear to go along with the order.

LIVING IN SUCHOWOLA ON our farm, my family was not in daily danger as were the Jews in Brody. There, able Jews had to work for Germans in factories for little or no pay. The main goal for everyone was to survive as best he could. If you worked at an important job, you received a special identity card that would save you from being taken by policemen at random to a labor camp. If a Gestapo man stopped a Jew, that Jew was lucky to get away alive. Because I had blond hair and blue eyes, and because I had learned to speak Polish fluently and without accent from my nanny in Brody, I felt that luck was on my side. Many other Jewish children spoke mainly Yiddish. Since they spoke Polish only occasionally, their inflection and accent were heavily Yiddish.

Therefore, if we needed supplies from Brody, I would drive a horse and wagon into the city. My mother would walk through the fields at a distance from me on the narrow roads, but we would meet in Brody. I did not wear my armband with the six-point star on it signifying I was a Jew. Instead, I acted like a Christian, crossing myself when I passed a cross because that was the custom of the local Poles and Ukrainians. I used to pass Jews working on the road, splitting rocks to pave the street. At times, I would spot my uncles, who were lawyers, engineers, and teachers before the war, now working in those road brigades doing hard labor. My heart would cry out, our eyes would meet, but I was too afraid to speak to them because I had to conceal my identity under the watchful eyes of the Ukrainian guards.

The Jews in Brody were under a curfew from six in the evening until four the next morning. They could not travel without a special permit, but it was easy for me to get in and out of Brody because of my "Aryan" looks. Well, it was easy, yes and no. I was a boy trying to do a man's work without bungling it. I remember one time, as I was crossing the railroad tracks with my horse and wagon to leave Brody for Suchowola, the crossing gates came down and I was caught right in the middle of the tracks. I just froze. I could hear the whistle of the train and voices shouting to me from behind the wagon, telling me to lift the gate. With my heart roaring, I jumped out of the wagon, pulled the horse, lifted the gate in front of us, and ran, flew, stumbled ahead. The train whistle was blowing wildly now, and one split second after I got wagon and all out of the way, a German troop train thundered past and the soldiers waved at me from the windows while I stood there, still frozen. The people who saw what had happened applauded me for my quickness and bravery, but even to this day, when I am in my car and hear a train whistle, something happens inside me, like a clamp closing my stomach.

And I remember another time. An old Jewish man, Chaim Strauss,

lived with his two daughters Fruma and Sara. He died, and his daughters asked my father for help in taking their father in his coffin to the Jewish cemetery in Pitkamin. My father asked the overseer's permission for
me to drive Mr. Strauss in his coffin in our horse and wagon. The two
daughters would be waiting at Pitkamin. I remember I felt frightened,
uncomfortable having a dead body so close to me, despite all the dead I
had seen sprawled on the streets of Brody. The world was upside down.

LIFE FOR THE JEWS in Brody was very hard. When I came to
Brody from the farm, I would bring food for our relatives, and it was
painful to find each time that more and more among them had disappeared in between those trips — either killed outright, or taken to labor
or death camps like Belzec or Majdanek.

And then, in Suchowola, word spread that the Friedmans would at
last be going to the ghetto. Many of our Christian neighbors were, I
know, secretly happy. Some offered to help transport us that evening.
We said our good-byes, thanked them, and told them we would leave in
the morning.

There were five hundred families living in Suchowola. Fifty of these
families were Polish Catholic nationals. The rest were Ukrainian Catholic and Russian Orthodox.

That October night was the darkest I can ever remember. There
was no moon and no stars. We disappeared into the inky blackness. We
ducked out of the farmhouse in the middle of the night. We took only
what we could carry on our backs. We knew the paths blindfolded. We
had rehearsed this many times, often under the nose of our overseer or
other Nazi collaborators.

My mother who, though I didn't yet know it, was about three months
pregnant, my brother Isaac, our teacher Sarah, and I hid in the attic of the
Symchucks' barn. Julia, one of their daughters, had saved my father from
the Gestapo. Now her family would hide us from the angel of death.

Only my mother knew where my father was hiding. This was in case
we were captured. Later I discovered that he had hidden in a neighbor's
hayloft. It was no more than a kilometer from our farmhouse.

The woman who hid my father was Maria Bazalchik. Her family was
made up of Ukrainians and practiced the Russian Orthodox religion. Her
brother was a Jew-hater, and her brother's son was the leader of the Ban-

deras, a Ukrainian terrorist group of the region. I believe that in 1947 he was killed by Russians. Mrs. Bazalchik had a crooked spine and her husband was somewhat retarded. So for many years, my father had helped them survive, and because Mrs. Bazalchik had a heart of gold and was very dedicated to her Christian beliefs, she now took my father in and kept it a secret from the rest of her family.

IT WAS A STRANGE LIFE, not really a life but a breathing space, in that loft above the animals. When I had to go to the bathroom, I would make a hole in the hay. The stench was awful, but because it was mixed with the rising odors of animal waste, we got used to the smell. After a while, we did not smell anything, and Mr. Symchuck in the morning would mix our waste with that of the animals.

The first morning was a shock because our area was very dark and the only light we got was from the cracks in the wood panels. At the end of the loft, we noticed a knot in the wood, and after a few days chipping away, we got a hole to the outside world and a welcome stream of daylight.

The Symchuck family was very close to us. The parents were both forty-six years old. Mr. Symchuck could not make a living on his little farm, so he worked also for my father on many different jobs. He was a skilled man, very quick to learn, especially in carpentry. Julia used to hang around my mother a lot, helping her sweep the store and do other tasks, and my mother would give her some extra money. So, knowing they needed extra resources to be able to help us, my father offered money and other valuables to the Symchucks if they would hide us. And they agreed to do so. These Ukrainian Christians took the chance, the risk, not knowing what they were getting themselves into. We had also prepared food to last us for six months.

Our hiding place was in the eastern portion of the attic. Hay separated us from the rest of the attic space. The "room" the four of us shared was about as big as a queen-size mattress. We were unable to stand up without hitting our heads. We lived day and night in our bed of hay, a single quilt covering us. My brother Isaac and I slept in one direction, my mother and Sarah slept in the other. We could speak only in whispers; otherwise, workers might hear us.

Living in the Brody ghetto was very hard, but it was better than what we had in our hiding place, not being able to stand up or go outside the little space we were crammed into. I used to think to myself that my father was not very smart to put us in this kind of situation because our lives were in danger. If the Ukrainian police found us, they would turn us over to the Gestapo, and those brutes would kill us or take us away to a camp. I did not like being cooped up with two women and a younger brother. I felt that if I were on the outside, I could manage on my own to pass as a Christian because many times before the war, my Christian friends would say to me, "You don't look at all Jewish," and working for two years on the farm had built up my muscles. In my inward thoughts, I hated my mother and my father because they were Jewish and I was paying for it by being their son.

I'd wanted to escape, but I was afraid to try. Earlier, we had heard reports of what was happening in Brody and the surrounding area — all the news of horror. Then I would hear stories of what had happened to Jews who were caught outside the ghetto, which would change my mind about running away. I used to be envious even of a horse's life — the horse was worked hard, but afterward it was given food and shelter, was groomed and curried, was given a chance to run on the pasture. It was not destined to be killed. The cows below us in the barn were given food so that they could give milk, and they were killed only when they could no longer give milk. I was willing to work, but I was not allowed to live. When I looked through the dollar-sized opening, I observed the storks that nested on the rooftops of the farm buildings. I wished that I were a stork with those strong wings — I could fly away to a place where I could fill my stomach, just so I would not be hungry all the time. The stork had no enemies, and I wondered what I had done to deserve this inhuman punishment. I sometimes dreamed of flying over the fields with a beautiful sunset on the horizon — until I was rudely awakened by gunfire outside. The Banderas used to train at night, firing their weapons. Night after night of harsh, metallic din. Whenever this gunfire woke me, I felt that I might be the next target of those bullets. These thoughts helped to prevent me from running away from my family and our unasked-for confinement. I feared being caught by the Banderas, those brutal, anti-Semitic Ukrainians, because they did not simply kill — they would cut off the penis or breasts of a Jew, torture their victim endlessly, then torch and bury the corpse.

So I felt sorry for myself most of the time. I would wake up to the same misery, hunger on more hunger, bones aching from the cold, not able to speak in a normal tone, obviously with nothing to laugh about, just to cry inside so no one would hear me. The best time I had was when I slept. Then my hunger pangs were not so bad and I was not bored to death by staring endlessly at the straw roof or at my mother, my brother, or the teacher, all of whom looked like living skeletons. It was painful even to look out the little hole and into the village where life was going on as usual: kids walking to school, farmers working in the fields, some older woman taking the cows to pasture, the rooster crowing and the other birds chirping away at one another — and there I was, stuck indoors and condemned to die.

At times when I was thinking of running away, I would visualize my relatives and their comfortable homes. Maybe they would allow me to visit. But for now, even they did not know where we were. We did not share this information with any of our relatives because it was a time when people looked out only for themselves, a time when humanity did not exist. Therefore, I did not know if my relatives were still alive or where to look for them. Whenever I planned an escape, all the negatives would come to my mind and persuade me that the attempt would be more dangerous than the danger I was in already.

Beyond these positive and negative thoughts, in the back of my mind was a feeling that my mother would protect me, that she would not let the Germans kill me. All these different ideas came to me, but I never shared them with my family; these thoughts of running away were what kept me going at times.

Occasionally we heard that some young Jews from the Brody ghetto had escaped and were fighting the Nazis with the partisans. I would think of my cousins, Heinach and Joseph. Heinach belonged to the poor side of the family, but he was not afraid of anybody. As a matter of fact, he had two teeth missing, knocked out in a fight. His family was too poor to replace them. But Heinach was always good to me and had always protected me, in and out of school.

So I thought of these cousins as being with the partisans, not afraid of the anti-Semites. I was sure that if they knew where I was, they would come and rescue me. The last time I saw Heinach was in September 1942, and Joseph in July 1942. Joseph was working in some kind of factory that

the Germans ran. He carried a special identity card that was supposed
to save him from the camps.

I HAD LOTS of fantasies. I would see Hitler in an animal cage being
taken from city to city, people throwing rotten tomatoes or eggs at him.
I would speak my fantasies in a whisper. I complained bitterly to my
mother.

"Why was I born a Jew?" I whispered. "If I hadn't been born to you,
I would be free." I fantasized that because I was blond and blue-eyed I
could have escaped. "He doesn't look like a Jew," people would say. But
people knew I am a Jew. Had I been a girl I could have escaped. They
would not be able to pull down my pants to identify me.

I spent most of my time lying on my back, counting the straws in the
roof. I was angry at the world. So many hours just lying there. When
I look back I can't understand how I survived and remained of sound
mind. We had with us a Hebrew prayer book, a *siddur*, which I read to
myself. I didn't understand the words, although I could read Hebrew
phonetically. I pretended that the words were God's language, that He
was listening to my prayers. Most of the time this was the only hope I
had, whispering to God in His language.

During the first three months we ate two meals a day: soup, bread,
and an occasional piece of meat. These would be shuttled up late at night
and in the early morning through a camouflaged opening in the loft. I
licked every pot clean with a vengeance. As the war dragged on, the meals
became fewer. Our six-months' supply dwindled and our portions were
cut by those who were hiding us. We then got only one meal a day, which
we received late at night and stored under the blanket, keeping it warm
with our bodies until morning, when we ate it for breakfast, lunch, and
dinner.

It was extremely cold, sometimes twenty below zero outside. In the
morning a thin layer of ice coated the quilt. Our hair often froze overnight. We could not wash. Our body oils and grit, at first an annoyance,
helped keep us warm. Today, it is hard to believe no one fell sick during
that time. A single cough or sneeze might have given us away. Isaac and
I passed the time killing fleas and lice.

Isaac wasn't growing. He was short enough to stand near the chim-

ney without banging his head. He would stand there for hours, whispering his fantasies to himself, seemingly oblivious.

I was the designated scout. There was a crawl space from the attic
passing above the Symchucks' living quarters. I would creep along and
listen for bits of information. Mrs. Symchuck was having an affair with
the chief of police. I enjoyed lying there with my erection, listening to
them make love. I also listened for news.

The chief told her that many people were suspicious and upset that
Jacob Friedman had not been seen behind the ghetto's barbed wire fence
with the other Jews, begging for bread in exchange for valuables.

"That son of a bitch Jacob," he said. "Why isn't he in there with the
rest of the Jews? Where can he and his family be? How did that crafty
old Jew escape?"

She never answered these questions.

To keep Mrs. Symchuck happy, we rewarded her with a pair of gold
earrings and other pieces of jewelry that we had stowed away. Mrs. Symchuck was an attractive woman, with black hair and a big bosom. She
was very proud of these earrings, especially since her husband struggled
to make a living.

Through our tiny peephole in the barn, we could see her outside
each day with the earrings on. Mother had begged her not to wear the
jewelry until after the war. Everyone knew she was having an affair with
the chief and must have assumed the jewelry was a gift from him. No
one suspected that we were hiding under their noses.

It came time for Mother to have her baby, and we faced a major
crisis. How would Mother give birth? Even if there were a doctor nearby,
we could not call him. And how could we control the infant's crying?
We argued back and forth what to do. If the baby were allowed to live,
our lives would be endangered. Mother had two boys and a third male
baby was stillborn in 1938. She desperately wanted to have a girl. We decided to vote, and the decision we made has haunted me ever since. I
wake in the middle of the night, crying. My brother still denies that he
voted. The baby would be suffocated by Sarah, who assisted with the
birth.

There was little room for Sarah to do much of anything except catch
the baby. Mrs. Symchuck sent up a bucket of hot water. She also brought
a burlap potato sack to hold the dead infant. Then she went quickly

away. Mother could not scream or allow herself to utter even a sound. I remember only that I saw her biting the quilt, white-faced. Isaac and I turned our backs. We never heard or saw a thing. Later we learned that the baby was a girl.

We had asked the Symchucks to bury the baby on our land. Mr. and Mrs. Symchuck that night took the body to be buried, but they had a hard time digging a hole deep enough because the ground was frozen. The month of March is still icy winter in Poland. And even though the night was pitch dark, they were afraid that someone might see them. They had to cover their tracks in the snow, and they were in a hurry to get home.

It was a miracle that my mother survived the birth process in our little hideaway. There was no medication for her, and we all slept in filth, infested with lice and fleas. How she escaped infection, I wonder to this day. It is hard to imagine what my mother and Sarah must have endured, and the Symchucks with their sad and terrible task. What would have happened if we had let the baby live, if we had taken a chance instead of having her suffocated? What would it have been like to have a sister? But as I remember the situation, I do not think my mother had any breast milk to feed the newborn. The baby would have starved, or if she did not starve, the lice would have eaten her up. Yet, when I think of that part of my life in 1943, the pain comes back to haunt me and I can never forgive the Nazis for what I was forced to be a part of at the age of fifteen — to take a life, just so I could survive. I have a problem when analyzing myself. Was I so terribly selfish then?

# Captivity
# and
# Liberation

I N MARCH 1943, ALMOST SIX MONTHS AFTER WE
went into hiding, I had a dream about my grandmother. It was sunset and I was in a rowboat on a swamp. The sun was huge as it set
on the horizon, and Grandmother appeared to speak to me. "Hershel,"
she said, "you know you are the oldest son. Our custom is that when the
oldest is thirteen he has to fast before the Passover, and tomorrow will be
Passover."

The vividness of the dream startled me. I was sweating heavily when
I told Mother and Sarah. They told me I should follow my grandmother's
advice. I fasted, sleeping more than usual to get through the hunger.
Mother and Sarah saved me some food to eat at the end of the day. The
strange part of this dream was that we didn't have a calendar to know the
day of Passover. When my mother shared my dream with Mrs. Symchuck,
she confirmed that it was in fact the right date, because the Jews in the
ghetto were preparing for Passover.

I used to have many scary dreams. In some I was chased through
a cornfield. In others, I was attacked by rats. But most of the dreams
concerned food, or the lack of it, and my terrible hunger. I would dream

of fish, chicken, potatoes, fruits, ice cream, but it was a nightmare, because chew as I might, I could not swallow this fictional food. These dreams were maddening.

By June 1943, a little less than a year after the ghetto's formation, Brody had been declared *Judenfrei*. No Jew was thought to be alive in Brody or in the surrounding towns and villages. Any Jew found would be shot on the spot. The same held true for anyone caught hiding a Jew. This was "the Law of Laws."

Thousands of our friends and neighbors had been transported from the Brody ghetto to concentration camps. Jewish residences within the ghetto had been burned to the ground. The liquidation of the ghetto took about a month, from May to June 1943, and we learned of the dreadful process from overhearing the Symchucks' conversations.

We wondered if there were other Jews still alive. After all, we had no idea who had escaped from the ghetto. Over the next several weeks we were horrified to hear tales of Jewish mothers who left their children behind or killed them so that they, the mothers, could survive. We also learned of children who left their parents to be shot. I did not believe such stories. I was certain Mrs. Symchuck was making them up. Had I believed them, I do not think I would be alive today. All my hope for survival would have been dashed. After we were liberated, we heard different stories, often from children whose parents had sacrificed their own lives to save them.

During the final days of the ghetto liquidation, one of the Ukrainian policemen who was helping the Germans returned to Suchowola and bragged that he had killed the Friedmans. We were happy to hear of this boast because it meant people wouldn't bother to search for us. Later, when others pressed this man for details of the Friedmans' deaths, he revealed that before the Ukrainian police would go into the ghetto, the Germans would fill them with liquor. He admitted that he had been drunk, and that the Friedmans he had killed might have been my mother's cousin and her two daughters rather than us. My mother's cousin had married a man named Friedman who was unrelated to my father.

As we listened to these stories, we thought to ourselves, "What good is it to be the only ones left, the only Jews alive?" Yet we clung to our life in that attic, miserable as it was.

Our food ration was down to one slice of bread per person each day.

My brother always saved bits to be eaten later. While he slept, I used to nibble at his slice. I reasoned that if he could sleep, he must not be as hungry as I. For a while, he believed the mice were eating his bread. This ruse went on for some time, until he awoke in the middle of a nap and caught me in the act. Even though he had to whisper, his anger shouted at me.

"You thief!" he said. "I can't believe you would do such a thing!"

"How could you steal from your own brother?" Mother said. "What kind of animal are you?"

"Why do you blame me?" I shot back. "It's all your fault. I didn't ask to be born a Jew. Look at me. I've got blond hair and blue eyes. I'm here for only one reason—you gave birth to me and you made me a Jew. That's the reason I'm suffering, so don't blame me for what I'm doing."

After that incident, Isaac guarded his bread closely. I still craved his portion, however, and I devised a scheme whereby I could earn some of it back.

"Look," I told him. "I'll tell you stories, and for every story I tell, you'll give me a bite of bread." I made up all kinds of imaginative tales. His favorite was hearing about how Hitler was caught and placed in a lion's cage. The cage was dragged by a wagon through the city and villages of Poland. Soon it would come to Brody and we would throw raw eggs and spit on the mustached tyrant. Isaac never tired of this, although I told it to him nearly every day.

When it came time for me to take my bite, he would hold his fingers over the bread to make sure I didn't take too big a portion. I bit his fingers so I could get a few extra crumbs. This game didn't last long, however. There was no more bread for any of us.

My brother and I also used to fantasize that after this war there would never be another war. We dreamed of bowls of soup with meat in it, of mashed potatoes and butter, of chicken and gefilte fish. These dreams were terrible because they made our hunger worse.

Sitting in my home today, it is difficult to believe how desperate we were and yet how tenaciously we clung to our miserable existence. I had blanked out this incident for many years. Only after watching a production of *The Diary of Anne Frank* did I remember that I, too, like one of the characters in the play, had been a thief who stole food from his own family.

Despite our competition for food, Isaac and I were close. I enjoyed listening to him whisper to himself. We loved to watch the mice. They would jump all over us. We were more afraid of them than they were of us. He and I would talk, and he would make up stories about the days to come when we would tell our children what had happened.

"No one would believe you, Isaac," Mother would say. "No human being can endure all this. I don't think we'll get through it." She was very depressed after the death of the baby.

We all became thinner and thinner. Now, as I continued my stealthy forays above Mrs. Symchuck's bedroom, eavesdropping on her trysts with the chief of police, listening for any news he might have of events affecting Jews in the surrounding area, I was too weak to get an erection. I remember thinking how bad this was, to be such a young man and already finished. But I could not discuss this with anyone.

AND WE CONTINUED to whisper amongst ourselves. We didn't know what had happened to Father. He was completely alone. He had his Bible, and he must have read it all the time. Mother would tell us stories from years past, how she loved to dance and carry on. Father tried to dance, but Mother said he couldn't manage a step.

Now all we could do was wonder about him. We marveled how he had known to trust our survival to these Ukrainians. Had he sought shelter from Poles, another minority hated by the Ukrainians, we might not have survived.

ONE NIGHT IN September 1943, I overheard a story about another Jewish family. A couple with a child were caught hiding in an underground grotto in a forest. A Ukrainian family who had previously hidden them reported them to the Ukrainian police in Suchowola. The Jews had run out of ransom money and had fled to a hiding place in the woods. Their "friends" promised to supply them with food but instead betrayed them, never letting on that they had once hidden them. The villagers of Suchowola were called out to witness the Jews' execution.

"Now watch this," one of the Ukrainian policemen said. "Any Jews, or anyone hiding a Jew, will meet with a similar fate."

First they undressed the woman and asked if anyone wanted her.

Mrs. Symchuck said she was very pretty. Since no one would lower himself to have sex in public with a Jew, not one person stepped forward. Her eight-year-old daughter stood by her mother's side. "The child screamed hysterically," Mrs. Symchuck said. "Most of the people laughed. The police shot the husband first, then the wife, and, in the end, the poor child."

That same night, after witnessing the execution, Mr. Symchuck got very drunk. I heard the argument from above. "Let's get rid of them," he yelled. "I can't stand them and I am not going to have my family killed because of these damned Jews!"

"As long as Jacob is alive, we can't," she said. "As long as he is alive, he will come and kill us."

"But our children agree with me," he shot back. "They want them dead, out of here." The children were terrified by the execution and by our hiding there. Their father's words set the littlest ones all to crying hysterically. They were too young to die, and after all, we were just crummy Jews. "We've risked our lives eleven months already. We will poison them," Mr. Symchuck said, "and that's that."

"But we can't," Mrs. Symchuck said. "Not yet."

I had heard enough. I crawled back to Mother and told her it was no longer safe for us to stay where we were. We had to leave. Father's hiding place was only a kilometer from ours. We hadn't seen him for eleven months. We had to sneak over that night, hunched and crouching on bent legs the entire way so as not to be seen. Every step of the way was filled with fear. In every shadow I saw a Ukrainian policeman. I bent over and hurried along, the fear in me so great I kept moving, trying to overcome the pain. I had either been sitting up or lying down for close to a year without using my leg muscles. My legs gave out from under me before we were halfway there. Mother carried me the rest of the way.

Father was shocked to see us. At first he was angry that we had attempted such a dangerous feat, but he was happy to see us alive. His hiding place was the size of a single bed. We all squeezed in and slept sitting up. He didn't get food on Mondays and Thursdays. Now there were four extra people sharing his meals.

The situation was impossible, but for a week, there we sat. The five of us could not have stayed any longer and survived. So Father gave Mother and Sarah his boots, his last worthy possessions, as a present for Mr. Symchuck, and he told them to go back to our previous hiding place.

"Tell Mr. Symchuck that if the Germans find you, he's to say that you're his sisters," he told Mother. "Without the boys, they'll have no way to prove you are Jewish. That should calm him down for a while."

Off they went, leaving Isaac, Father, and me in this little hole, eating barely enough food for one person.

ONE HAS TO understand Mr. Symchuck's dilemma. When he originally took us in, it was for humane reasons: a good human being should help another human being who has been kind to him and his family for so many years. Mr. Symchuck was also getting financial rewards, so he was getting double the good fortune for doing the right thing. But after he saw with his own eyes the brutality of the police in killing some helpless Jews, he realized that he was jeopardizing the lives of his own family.

The Symchucks were God-fearing people and kind Christians, but the liquor Mr. Symchuck drank influenced him badly, pushing forward evil thoughts. These, combined with fear, made him consider poisoning us. But the fact that, a few days later, he let the women return showed that Mr. Symchuck had, in the end, a good heart.

AT FATHER'S PLACE, we were within earshot of a well-traveled road, so we listened intently to overhear whatever we could. One evening Father heard the Banderas marching toward our hiding place and he assumed we had been discovered. He took out his razor blade and prepared to slit our throats. "We will not be tortured," he whispered to Isaac and me. "Otherwise, we will give away your mother and Sarah."

"I haven't done anything wrong," Isaac cried. "I shouldn't have to die. I haven't harmed anyone. Besides, if they are going to kill me, at least they should feed me first so I can die on a full stomach. If you want to die, go ahead, but don't kill me too." I don't remember what I had to say. I just remember being so scared.

The Banderas beat up the Polish farmer next door very badly. They never bothered to search our barn, however. The woman who hid father was the aunt of the local Bandera leader. The thugs assumed she wouldn't be hiding anyone. She had not told even her husband or two sons. Father had chosen exactly the right place, but we didn't feel safe anymore.

There seemed to be no end to the war. The Russians were advancing slowly and then stalling. Father was depressed. He didn't see a solution to our desperate plight. He considered burning the village to the ground. He didn't care if we all perished in the fire.

Often, he would lose himself in prayer, which was his only source of hope. Now he forced us to pray with him.

"Father, you constantly pray for the Russians to win, yet they are atheists," I told him. "They don't believe in God, or anything like the God we believe in."

He slapped my face.

"A Jew must first learn the Torah, the Mishnah, and the Gemara," he said. "If, after all that study, he is convinced there is no God, he can be an atheist without sin. But an ignoramus like you has no business questioning God's wisdom."

We became more desperate. We knew the Germans were being pushed back, but our existence was too precarious for us to survive much longer.

In my father's tiny, cramped place, we were in almost complete darkness except for light shining through the cracks. At least at the Symchucks' place, we had that hole in the wood. Through it, we could see what was happening in the outside world.

We mostly slept at my father's place, and I got weaker and weaker. The shortage of nourishment affected me more than it did my father and my little brother, maybe because of my age — fifteen and a half, a prime growth age. There were days I hoped I would not wake up, but other days I would be afraid to go to sleep, fearing I would not wake up to see liberation.

The months that I spent with my father, September till December 1943, were the worst months of my life. The space was so small that our bodies were always touching. It was the most inhuman environment for starving humans to endure. The worst part of all was not being able to talk with my father — we were to remain utterly silent, except to pray. For these three months, all I did was pray and sleep, pray in a language that I did not understand, pray to a God who at that time I was afraid had abandoned the Jewish people and closed His eyes and ears to their suffering. But, being stuck in this miserable space, I had no choice but to pray, because that was the only way to communicate, and it gave me some hope.

At the Symchucks' we were right on the main road that went from Brody to Tarnopol. My father's place, however, was a quarter mile or more from any road, so not only did we spend most of our time in semi-darkness but no outside news came our way. Mrs. Bazalchik was not a very talkative woman. One time we heard her husband yell at her that he was going to report her to the police because she had a Jewish ax that had belonged to Jacob Friedman. Mr. Bazalchik was retarded and child-like. Right next to the farm lived another farmer who was Polish, but his wife was Ukrainian. Our two barns almost touched each other; however, these neighbors did not talk much with one another.

In the Symchucks' attic, I could peek through the hole and observe the birds and how happily they would jump from one branch to another. I would fantasize that I, too, was a bird and could fly to the river and bathe in the fresh, clean water. But from my father's place, I saw nothing except the Hebrew letters in the book I prayed from. It had been over a year since I had bathed in water, in October 1942. Now my skin was full of small round circles, the result of flea bites. What little blood I had, the fleas sucked on. Right below where we slept was a chicken coop; at night the chickens would gather to sleep and lay their eggs.

I was already skin and bones when we arrived at my father's place, but here the conditions were much worse than at the Symchucks'. All of us — my little brother Isaac, Father, and I — were starving to death.

By December 1943, it was clear that the three of us could not survive on the scraps of food Mrs. Bazalchik was giving us. It was decided that I would go to stay with Mother, in secret, without telling the Symchucks. That way Isaac could have more food, and I could share the food Mother and Sarah were eating. Father would take me over there, leaving Isaac alone for a short time.

It was going to be dangerous to walk in the snow because of our tracks and the crunchy sound. There was a curfew from 6 p.m. to 6 a.m. We might be captured by the German patrols who were scouting the countryside for Jews by day, or by the Banderas bandits who controlled the village at night. The two groups had a kind of truce — you don't attack me and I won't attack you — but we, the unarmed, defenseless Jews, had no leverage. Both groups wanted to kill us. Even with the danger and un-certainty, my father had to take this risk because our lives were hanging by a thread.

We covered our feet in rags to absorb their sound on the snow. Father slid down from the loft, and I followed. When I landed on the ground, however, my legs collapsed like rubber. There was no strength left in them. Father had to carry me. Every second of the dark journey was fear-some. When we got to Mother's hideout, we saw that the Germans had put up a field kitchen right in front of the house. We approached from the back, and just as we crawled into Mother's hiding place, a German patrol passed. A split second later and we would have been caught. God must have watched over us that night. An angel, perhaps Elijah, must have blinded our enemy's vision. Father exchanged a few words with Mother, hugged her, then disappeared in the darkness of the night. We wondered if we would ever see him again.

Now Mother, Sarah, and I were together, and Isaac was with Father, who managed to return undetected to his original hideout. I missed Isaac.

THE HUNGARIAN TROOPS that had helped the Germans in the area were retreating. This was early in 1944. Their departure was a clear sign of Russian progress in the war. Soon the Germans would leave the area too. Mrs. Symchuck couldn't wait to tell Mother and Sarah. It was the first good news in a year, and she wanted to tell them face-to-face.

They hid me under the quilt, still not wanting to let her know I was there. They sat on top of me, and thank God they were not that heavy. Mrs. Symchuck kept repeating herself. "They're leaving," she said. "They're going." Mother and Sarah nodded yes.

"I can't believe it. I can't believe it."

I listened, half-crushed and choking for air. By the time Mrs. Sym-chuck finished talking and left, I was almost unconscious.

OUR HIDING PLACE sat on a hill near the highway. Through a peephole one night we saw the entire village ablaze, all of the Polish farms and houses. The retreat of the Germans had left a clear field for the Banderas. They went about their business of massacring Poles. They cut off women's breasts. They threw priests and other men into wells. With the full moon, the fires made it look like bright daylight. The Banderas seemed to have gone berserk, killing every Pole they got their hands on. I had never heard or seen such wailing, and I hope to God I never do again.

The Banderas had begun as part of the so-called Organization of Ukrainian Nationalists (OUN), a Fascist revolutionary sect with a long history of Jew-hating, dating back to a man named Petlura who started his own pogroms in 1916. Stephan Bandera, a Ukrainian born in Poland, was their present-day leader. He had been arrested by Polish police in 1938 and 1939 for burning Jewish property. When the Germans came in 1941, Bandera helped kill the Jews. At night he and his followers murdered Jews, and the Germans didn't interfere. Later, when Bandera realized the Germans were no more interested in a free Ukraine than the Russians or Poles had been, he began to organize his own group, who called themselves Banderas. As the Germans started losing the war, his guerrillas seized property and positioned themselves for the end. They killed both Poles and Jews, in order to take over property. OUN leaders claim that in 1944 Bandera formed the Anti-Bolshevik Block of the Nations (ABN) to unite all the non-Russian minorities working for the Third Reich, and even after the war, Bandera led a guerrilla uprising against the Russian communists, who later found him in Germany and assassinated him.*

The Banderas were now desperate to find Jacob Friedman. Nearly every prominent Jewish man in the area around Brody had been accounted for, except Father. Even the baby had been found, her burial ground on our former property having been uncovered by a pair of dogs. We were all shocked. I was so upset by the image of dogs dragging my baby sister along the ground that I vomited. The discovery of the baby's remains provided the Ukrainians with further evidence that the rest of our family might still be alive.

The Russians were closing in now, and we looked forward to hearing their planes fly overhead. In February 1944, a caravan of trucks drove into the village and a hundred or more German soldiers stepped out. They were retreating toward Germany and intended to take everything in sight. The Symchucks had left the previous night with their possessions

*See "Report of October 1945," USNA, RG 226 Record of the Office of Strategic Service, XL24218.

to hide in the forest. They had gotten wind of what the Germans were planning and knew that if we were found, it would be the end of them.

The first group of Germans came, knocked on the barn door, and left. We held our breaths. A second group came banging and Mother whispered her prayers. Twenty to thirty minutes later, a third group came pounding and probing. I was so scared I wet my pants.

"We'd better go," one of them said. "Somebody important lives in this house." They didn't search for us, thinking the barn and house belonged to a Ukrainian national cooperating with the Germans.

Again God seemed to be watching over us. The Germans broke into every house except our shelter and looted everything in sight except the Symchucks' house.

A day passed without food, then another. I was skin and bones. We were starving. Then one day I thought I heard somebody coming up to the loft. I thought it must have been Mrs. Symchuck coming back to bring us something to eat. I crawled to the opening to reach for the food. This time I saw a bayonet in my face, and I froze. Suddenly I heard Mrs. Symchuck's voice from below.

"What do you want?" she asked.

"I am looking for some eggs," the soldier said.

"Oh no, don't go up there," she said. "I will give you some eggs."

LATER IN FEBRUARY we could hear the artillery fire in the distance. It was music to our ears. Every day the music got closer. We had heard the Russians were only forty kilometers from the village. For the first time we could see the Germans losing, retreating in torn clothing. I relished the mud on their boots, the filth on their uniforms. They had always seemed ten feet tall to me. Now they were whittled down to size.

On March 13, 1944, the Germans were pushed out of Suchowola by the Russians. The attack started before first light and the battle continued most of the day. We heard Russian spoken outside the barn and could see Russian soldiers firing from concealed positions. We could barely contain our glee, yet we didn't know what would happen to us. We were scared. My first thoughts were of the abandoned German army kitchen. I can still remember the smells of cooked goulash. I couldn't remember when I had last tasted meat. I didn't care if the Germans came back tomorrow so long as I could eat their food today.

Mrs. Symchuck brought each of us a plate of goulash, still warm. We ate it ferociously, and a loaf of bread. Mother climbed down from the loft to talk to Mrs. Symchuck about getting us some water. Her husband and children were still in hiding, but she had the courage to come back and care for her house and for us. Eating the stew made us very thirsty, so thirsty that Sarah and I began to cry. Outside the Russians were still shooting at the retreating Germans.

"I'm going to die," I said.

"A taste of freedom has made you crazy," Mother said.

"But we've had no water," I begged. "Can't we please have some water?"

"There is nothing we can do about it," Mother said. "We can't get to the well."

It was difficult to sleep that night because we were so thirsty and scared. My throat was parched and my face caked with salt. Before dawn we were shocked to hear German voices. I wanted to climb down and run for some nearby rifles that the Germans had left near the field kitchen, but Sarah stopped me. I was so weak I could not have picked up a rifle. Nor did I know how to shoot one. We were completely distressed by the presence of the Germans. Where had they come from? What were they going to do? My first thought was that they had returned and routed the Russians. This time they would kill us, too.

"We should have told the Russians we were here," Sarah whispered. "Now it is too late."

"I must get to the rifles," I told her.

"No," she said. "You'll give us away."

That was the longest night of my life.

Later in the morning we heard Russian voices. They had discovered the Germans hiding in the hay immediately below us in the barn. Mr. Symchuck stood beside a group of Russian soldiers.

"Let's kill this bastard," a Russian said, pointing to Mr. Symchuck. "He's been hiding Germans!"

"Come down," Mrs. Symchuck yelled out to us.

We immediately jumped down from the loft. Sarah spoke Russian and explained to them what had happened. In the end, we saved the poor farmer's life. The Russian commander of the battalion that took Suchowola was called into the barn.

"Jews!" the commander said. "I can hardly believe my eyes. I've seen no Jews in months, not since leaving Stalingrad."

"What's the big deal?" one of his men remarked. "Why should we honor Jews?"

"What unit are you from?" the commander shot back.

"I'm far from my unit," the soldier said.

"Arrest him," the commander told two of his bodyguards.

We were astonished to see such action taken on our behalf.

The commander, who also happened to be Jewish, had his orderly bring bread and sardines to us and his men to celebrate our liberation. His men stared at my skeletal body as I gulped down the food.

Because we looked like creatures from another planet, the Russians asked us to undress and they burned our clothes. They cut away our hair and sprayed us with some kind of powder. All the months in hiding, we had not been able to wash ourselves or change our bedding or the clothes we wore and also slept in. We had only enough water to drink, one bucketful that had to last us for days. In the winter this water was coated with a thin sheet of ice. When the Russian officer saw how yellow my teeth were, he could not believe his eyes.

As we celebrated with the Russian commander and his troops, we did not even have time to speak of Father and Isaac, because by noon the German planes started bombing again.

We immediately ran to Father's hideout. When we got to where we thought it was, we saw a big bomb crater in the middle of the yard. The barn had collapsed. We searched the rubble for signs of them. Nothing. It was March and the temperature had fallen to below zero. We kept searching. In the farmhouse we found two dead soldiers, one Russian, the other German.

We ran outside and headed toward the river. We were astounded to see Isaac and Father huddled beneath a bridge, which the Germans were now bombing. Father had rags wrapped around his feet. I thought he must have finally lost his mind. Why was he hiding under a targeted bridge?

"We must get out of here," Mother screamed. "Hurry!"

They ran up an embankment to meet us. As we ran for shelter, Father pulled a pair of boots for himself from a dead German soldier. Soon, Isaac and I had boots on our feet, too. We found a loose horse and hooked him up to a sled. As it grew dark, we made our way into the village center.

We bedded down in an abandoned house. Before long we were joined by some Russian soldiers.

We woke early the next morning and headed for the farm to get some food. We used to keep potatoes under the ground during the wintertime so they would not get frozen. To our delight, they were still there.

As we loaded the sacks of potatoes on the sled, I began to feel the life leaving my limbs. Finally I couldn't lift or even walk another step. At the time I thought it was because I had been kneeling down on the snow and ice for hours. Father encouraged me to keep trying to walk. But I couldn't even stand for very long. Then he made me some crutches out of big sticks.

The village was empty of civilians. We could see only Russian soldiers and other scavengers like us, going from house to house and eating food that was left behind. Just as we left one house, a bomb leveled it. Our hunger made us oblivious to the bombs. We just didn't hear them dropping.

Isaac and I could no longer walk. "Sit in the house over there," Father told us. "Sit beside a table and crawl under it when the bombs drop." Mother and Sarah went running to see if they could find some flour, eggs, or even a chicken, anything besides potatoes.

After about an hour, a German plane strafed the ground with bombs. They exploded all around us. Isaac and I were frightened. It was the first time we had been left alone since we went into hiding. No one was there to tell us what to do. Isaac climbed on my back and we crawled out of the house into a cellar. It was dark and damp.

Later when Father returned, we could hear him yelling for us from where he had left us. I began to cry. Why had he left us alone? Now he'd never find us. When he somehow managed to find his way into the cellar, I was in tears, shaking.

"Get hold of yourself," he said. "You're almost sixteen years old. You have to learn to stand on your own two feet and take care of yourself. Let's go." We traveled by sled toward Pitkamin, about ten kilometers from Suchowola. We arrived near sunset. The civilian population, Ukraines and Poles, were scattered across the snow like ants. We asked the first people we saw whether they knew of any Jews left alive in the city. No one seemed to know. We asked some Russians, and they pointed out to us a house where they said some Jews were gathered. When we got there, the house was deserted, but some potatoes were left behind. By now we were very hungry. Mother and Sarah's search for food had been futile.

Father started a fire in the oven and we baked potatoes. We ate them without salt or butter and then we fell asleep. The following morning, Father spoke with a group of soldiers.

"You'd better retreat farther from the lines," a lieutenant said. We immediately set out on our horse-driven sled across the snow.

It was just before Orthodox Easter. Although I could not walk, we stopped at houses on the way and I used my crutches to get to the front door. I greeted the owner of each house cheerily.

"Jesus Christ was great," I said. I held out a little sack for food. Some of the farmers gave me Easter eggs, and we lived on these as we retreated from Suchowola. Mother joined me in praising Jesus for handouts.

It was slow going to Pitchayew. We slept in barns and wrapped straw around us at night to keep warm. We never felt safe when admitting that we were Jews. I hadn't walked now since being liberated. In Pitchayew we found a Russian Jewish doctor to examine my legs. He diagnosed arthritis and suggested that little could be done. He told me I would probably never walk again and sent me to the local Russian military hospital for a thorough examination. He was concerned, as we all were, about the possibility of my contracting typhus.

When I arrived at the hospital, my temperature was 104 degrees. I did indeed have the dreaded typhus, which spread in epidemic numbers, wiping out eighty-five percent of its victims. Fortunately the military hospitals were well equipped to deal with the disease, much more so than were the civilian hospitals. I received the proper medication, which at least gave me a chance. I remember sweating profusely for what seemed like days. Once the fever broke, my appetite returned.

My doctor saw that I was given three carefully prepared meals a day. He also gave me exercises for my legs. They hurt so much that I wanted to die. My Jewish physician, however, was determined not to let me die, or to let me become a cripple for the rest of my life.

We were not yet even settled in Pitchayew when, in the middle of the night, the Russians came and took Father away to the Russian army. They didn't care about what we had been through. They simply conscripted all men under the age of fifty-five. So he was dragged into the army, his feet swollen and his body tired. He was taken about eighty kilometers away for basic training and was gone for six months with a supply unit.

Mother and Isaac also came down with typhus and were in the same hospital with me. Thank God, we all survived. When I left the hospital a month after my admission, I walked out on my own two feet. I went to work in the Russian army kitchen and ate as much as I could all day long. I would bring home gallons of fresh soup each day and even managed to take some meat. We lived in a barn at the time, and without this food we would all have starved.

During our stay in Pitchayew we met two Jewish orphans, a brother and sister. The boy had been saved because a doctor had added a foreskin to his penis just before the German occupation. The two children then posed as non-Jews, helping the partisan guerrillas.

Besides my family, those two were the only Jews we knew then to have survived the Nazis. So, for our time in Pitchayew, we were like a family, sharing an abandoned apartment and trying to get our strength back. We waited to hear that Brody was liberated so that we could go back home, not knowing what Brody would look like anymore. We again lived from day to day, trying to get by.

I continued to work in the Russian kitchen. Mother worked on some nearby farms. We stayed in Pitchayew for three months, until we heard that the Russians had captured Brody on June 10, 1944. We immediately packed our belongings to return. Before leaving, we traded our sled for a horse-driven wagon.

When we arrived in Brody, I was shocked to find none of our relatives. When I was in hiding, I had feared that I would be the only Jew who survived. A terrible, empty feeling came over me at the loss of so many cousins, and I felt as though I were standing all alone in a huge stadium. Never before had I been in such a dreary situation.

Then we found my cousin Pepe, the only one of my father's relatives to survive the Nazi terror. It was like finding a priceless treasure. Pepe was the daughter of my father's sister, Freda Strouse, who had lived in Ferlajuwka in a neighboring house on the same parcel of farmland with my uncle Salomon and his family. Aunt Freda and Uncle Abraham had had a son and two daughters, Anschul, Pepe, and Yite. Grandma Klara had lived with Uncle Salomon.

Pepe Strouse was the eldest of Freda's three children. She told us that the German and Ukrainian police came to take my cousin Anschul away, but Grandma Klara poured scalding water from the upstairs window onto the police and told Anschul to run. They killed my cousin Anschul and burned my grandma to death in her own house. Pepe survived the 1941 pogrom in Zlotchiw, during the first week of the Nazi occupation. She fell beneath the bodies of other Jews as they were machine-gunned by the edge of a mass grave in a ravine bordering the city. That night, after the shooting had stopped, she dug herself out and fled. A Ukrainian priest's wife hid Pepe and risked her family to save a Jew. During Pepe's visit with us, she sought my parents' advice about whether she should marry the priest's eldest son, who had fallen in love with her. Though she was forever grateful to his family, she did not love him, nor did she want to change her religion. After talking with my parents, Pepe left for Lvov. There she later met and married a man named Joseph, with whom she left Russia for Poland.

While Pepe was with us, we heard tragic stories. All we could do was cry in sorrow, remembering happy times we had once had with people we loved who were now gone. We learned that nearly four hundred Jews had been hidden from March 14 to June 10, 1944, the three months prior to the liberation of Brody. They lived in underground tunnels, sewers, or in hideouts as we had. Over three hundred of them were discovered and shot by Germans, or were killed by artillery shells in the final days of the occupation.

The city of Brody was in ruins, with seventy percent of its buildings destroyed. Brody had been a railroad hub, and its highway led to Lvov, the next major city. It had been important for the Germans to maintain control of this junction city as long as possible so that they could build the next defense line and hold the Russians outside the city for three months.

There was no running water or electricity, so for our lights we used empty shell casings. Each of these stood about fifteen inches high, with a wick made from pieces of blanket. A hole on one side of the casing drew in air and drew up the kerosene, because the top was squeezed to hold the wick in place. Often, by accident, someone would knock the shell casing over, and we then had a fire on our hands. The first time this happened, we threw water on the fire, which only made it burn higher. A

Russian soldier standing nearby helped us to put it out by throwing a blanket over it; otherwise, we might have gone up in smoke! But, gaining knowledge from this kind of "life in the wilds" training, we were able to handle the accidental fires with much more ease after that.

With Father in the army, Mother now took charge. Before the war, she had been accustomed to having a maid. She did, of course, manage the textile store, but Father ruled all our affairs. She never had to think much about money. Suddenly, the decisions concerning our survival fell on her shoulders alone.

She plunged into her new role with enthusiasm. One of the first things she did was to buy homemade vodka from the farmers and resell it at a profit to the Russian soldiers. She also hitchhiked by herself to Lvov, approximately one hundred kilometers from Brody, where she purchased salt and supplies, which she, in turn, traded at the Brody farmers' market.

Before the war nearly fifteen thousand Jews had lived in Brody, including its surrounding area. Now there were fewer than one hundred survivors. We were elated, however, to see any other Jew left alive. We had thought we were the only survivors. We were in fact the only nuclear family to have survived intact. The few other Jews were now mostly orphans.

Somehow we found a place to live, on a street named Happy Street. We had two rooms in a house that was used as a commune. Fifteen other people lived in the Kolchoz commune. We were all Jews, all women, except for a man who had lost his arm fighting as a partisan, and my brother and me

Before the war, we knew only a few of the one hundred Jews who lived in Brody in 1944. Some of these survivors had not lived in Brody in prewar days. Now, however, we all became like a family. Of relatives who had survived, we knew then only of my cousin Pepe and my uncle Salomon, who was with the Russian army. Of my Gentile friends, boys who had been classmates before the war, those who were Ukrainian were in the Banderas underground; those who were Polish nationals had either been killed by the Banderas or had moved away to Lvov.

Mother sold the horse and wagon. We earned our food and whatever little money we had by selling liquor to soldiers. Again, Mother would trade with the farmers for their vodka, home made from potatoes and yeast. They used to mash it, let it sit for three days, and then boil it. What a stink it made! Still, it was the only spirit available and we made a nice profit from selling it. Our quarters became like a tavern, because Mother was one of the few suppliers of vodka.

My teeth hurt, but I was reluctant to see a dentist because they were all yellow. In hiding, I had not been able to take care of my teeth. The dentist told me she had never seen such neglect; it took her months to scrape off the yellow. My gums bled constantly. In Russia they didn't give you any painkillers, so tears would roll down my face. Whenever I went to see the dentist, I was in pain before I even sat down in the chair.

Sarah now took care of the household. Isaac and I started school again. I also became head of a young communist group called Komsomol. I made many friends and quickly became a big shot. Mother saw to it that I wore handsome clothes by purchasing officers' uniforms and then tailoring them for me. I had regained most of my weight and wore a pair of fancy Russian leather boots.

According to Mother, I was the handsomest boy around. Best of all, I looked older than my age.

# My New
# Hobby

**M**Y FIRST SEXUAL ENCOUNTER WAS WITH
Ninochka, a schoolteacher who also happened to be the assistant principal. She had light brown hair, stood about five
foot three, and was in her late twenties. I was sixteen at the time. Although I had always been a good student, I wasn't doing that well now
because I had missed three school years during the German occupation.

Ninochka, who was unmarried, invited me to her flat near the
school for the weekend to chop wood in exchange for some tutoring. This
was in the fall of 1944. The weather was cold, and we had made a fire to
keep warm.

We sat on the floor in front of the fire, and before I knew it she was
kissing me passionately. My blood started to boil. This feeling was like
nothing I had ever imagined. My reaction to listening to Mrs. Symchuck
and the police chief paled by comparison. When she reached to put my
hand on her breast, I was on fire. Then she undressed me. She had only
a robe on, which she quickly slipped off. I had never seen such a beautiful body in my entire life or imagined that any woman could be that
pretty. I remember being entranced by her breasts.

She took me by the hand into the bedroom; my feet seemed not to touch the floor. She started kissing my lips and shoulders with her tongue, and we fell onto the bed.

We never said a word to each other. I knew very little about how to touch a woman, but she gently showed me. She took my face and guided it to her left breast. I kissed it, and following her lead I began to nibble and then to suck. She became wild and guided my penis into her. I felt a warmth and pleasure beyond anything I had ever known. I began pushing into her like an animal, but she didn't seem to mind. With each thrust she seemed to hold me tighter. I didn't know what was happening. It went on like that for three or four minutes. Before I knew what had happened, it was over.

I was very embarrassed. Everything had happened so fast. I'd had no education in sex up to that time, nor had I seen any books or had any discussions. My parents never talked to me about it. Without my knowing it, Ninochka had made a man out of me.

I felt like a tiger who had been let out of a cage. Our affair went on for about ten weeks and then came to a dangerous end. We were resting on the bed after one of our sessions when we heard footsteps on the stairs leading up to her apartment. In marched Ninochka's boyfriend, a six-foot-tall Russian major. He was about forty years old, with a gun in his holster. Ninochka jumped out of bed like a bullet. She begged him to spare our lives.

"He's just a boy!" she cried.

I got dressed as fast as I could. Then I ran out the door. I never saw Ninochka intimately again. Besides teaching me about sex, she had helped me to learn that making love to a woman can be dangerous. But my appetite was now whetted, and there was no stopping me.

Our family's two-room flat with its large living room and open kitchen area was now a kind of gathering place, almost a tavern, where soldiers temporarily became friends of the family and talked about the war. A female second lieutenant came in one night with a group of soldiers, and somehow I ended up walking her back to the barracks.

She took me to a warehouse full of folded parachutes. She slept on a narrow bed in the corner of this cold room. We started kissing and tried clumsily to undress each other in the dark. I dropped my pants without undressing all the way. Being more experienced now, I knew what to do.

Because of the war, there was a shortage of physically capable men around. This was fine with me, as older women like Ninochka and the lieutenant were hungry for love. I was more than willing to oblige them. My peers at school resented my running around, though. Girls my own age were especially annoyed. I walked into class some days to discover a funny drawing of me on the blackboard. I was often depicted trimming my eyebrows, a feature I took pride in. I had very little to do with the girls at school, preferring older women. I dressed in an officer's uniform and looked and acted more mature. Even if my peers at school resented me, I didn't care.

I saw life quite differently from them. I had lived in enforced captivity for over three years while they had been free. Now that I had tasted sex, I was driven by it. I felt that I was a man and they were adolescents. School bored me and seemed like an intrusion upon my personal freedom. I became best friends with a boy named Moses, from Brody. He and his father had hidden with a Christian Polish woman whom his father ended up marrying after the liberation. Moses did not like his stepmother, even though she had saved his life. He was even more rebellious than I was. Both of us refused to take orders from our mothers. We felt that we no longer needed them.

Once Moses and I started home after one in the morning, way past curfew. We were afraid of getting shot. We had on our Russian uniforms and began walking the poorly lit streets as if we owned them. We ran into a patrol and challenged the soldiers before they challenged us. It worked. They gave us their passwords, not asking for ours. From then on we were safe.

When I finally made it back to our flat, I knocked on the door. Mother, who was awake, slowly opened it. She had heard some soldiers walking past the window earlier who spoke of a young guy getting killed. She was sure they were speaking of me. My flashlight shown on her. She was angry and held a broom in one hand. I could see what she wanted to do with it and went back outside to wait for her to go to sleep.

"You're not marching in the May Day parade," she said to me the next morning.

"But I'm too old to be punished," I shot back.

"The hell you are," she said.

"But I'm supposed to march in that parade. Komsomol is counting on my leading them."

"Too bad," she said. "You should have thought of that last night."

Some very long days followed. The thought of missing the parade depressed me. I went to Mother and apologized for making her suffer that night.

"Will you not make me suffer again?"

"I promise."

"We'll see," she said.

On the day of the parade she relented. She had prepared my uniform for me to march.

Mother and Sarah returned to Suchowola in the fall of 1944. This was their first visit since the liberation, and Mother's purpose was to reclaim the valuables we had entrusted to the care of a couple of Ukrainian families before the Russians took over our store and house in Brody. But she was told by them that the Germans had dug up all our possessions, or that, because the front line stopped in Suchowola, the Russians had found every one of our treasures—this from people who had been our trusted friends before the war. It was good foresight on my father's part not to have asked these families to hide us. Anyway, by the time my mother got finished chatting and visiting with these so-called friends, it was getting dark. It was not safe to travel back to Brody. The mayor of the village invited Mother and Sarah to spend the night with his family. During the night, there was a pounding on the mayor's door. The Banderas had come to kill Mother and Sarah. The mayor said they would have to kill him first. He did not back down. He saved their lives. My mother never returned to Suchowola again.

IN SEPTEMBER 1944 FATHER paid us a visit without notice. I don't remember how he managed to get to Brody, but he was there for two days, just long enough to get Mother pregnant.

I was so embarrassed. I was sixteen, sexually active myself, and now Mother, at age forty-two, was pregnant. I also didn't look forward to sharing Mother with a baby brother or sister. The thought of such competition rattled me. It also seemed stupid to me that she would consider having another child at her age.

My feelings were hurt and I lost all respect for women. My motto became "Love women, be loved by many women, but never again let a woman get close enough to hurt me." I continued to live only for the moment. Although only sixteen, I tried to act as if I were thirty. Some days I would sleep with three different women. One girl told me that by the time I was thirty I would be worn out and incapable of having sex.

Although the Soviet army was in control of Brody during the day, the Banderas ruled at night. It was a constant battle. They murdered at least twenty of the surviving one hundred Jews.

Moses and I spent a lot of time on the streets. The entire ghetto had crumbled, except for the old Great Synagogue. Its roof was gone, but its walls still stood. Sometimes Moses and I would go into its ruins and close our eyes. We'd sit against a wall and remember how beautiful the synagogue was before Hitler. We could hear the voices of dead worshipers cry out to us, and we were frightened by the echoes.

This was before Easter 1945. The Banderas had killed a Polish child and then wrapped the body with barbed wire and left it in the old synagogue. They put out rumors that Jews had killed the child to use the blood to make matzoh. The case was investigated by a Jewish police officer, who found the Ukrainians responsible. The Banderas, however, continued to blame the Jews, calling it a "ritual murder."

Father was now with the Polish army, fighting on German soil. This was good news to me. He would have an opportunity to confront the Germans directly. I kept my joy within, however, because I was ashamed that Father was in the Polish army. I would have preferred that he fight in the Soviet army. I was still a young communist and the head of Komsomol. I had been elected by chance, with no previous organizational experience. I knew that I had power and I quickly abused my position.

There were ten members in our group. A close friend was a boy named Misha. The woman in charge, Comrade Konjew, was about thirty. She was very heavy, and though she tried to seduce me on occasion, I resisted at all cost. Before long we grew to sixty members, and Misha became my assistant.

Volunteer work was the basis of party discipline. I started to organize weekends for schoolchildren to stack old bricks to be used in rebuilding Brody. We also cleaned up the streets. The project was a big success, but our good deeds were not appreciated by anyone. Other projects demanded more and more initiative, but I lost interest and pursued my other hobby.

Comrade Konjew began to dislike me as I spent more of my time making love to girls. She plotted to unseat me from my position. At a meeting Misha spoke out against me. That day I was unseated as head of the Komsomol party, and Misha was elected to my post.

I felt betrayed. The party still perceived me as an ambitious and smart young man, but in need of lots of polishing. The party leadership decided to send me to a Russian officers' school. It was named after Kutozow, the famed Russian general who fought Napoleon.

When I told Mother I was elected to officers' school, she started to cry. She had been receiving letters from Father, who would soon be discharged from the army. He had convinced her to leave the Ukraine, now under Soviet rule, for Silesia, a part of Poland that used to be German but was now called West Poland. We had never accepted Russian citizenship. We considered ourselves to be Polish citizens. After the war, the Russians signed an agreement with Poland to unite families that had been separated by the war. Those who wished to live as Polish citizens would be permitted to leave Russia for Poland.

"How can I tell your father I left without you?" she said.

Moses's father visited me. "Your mother treats you like a king," he said. "At military school you will be eating black bread and water. You'll probably die there from hunger. You'll be sleeping on the floor rather than on a bed."

Mother had made sure I was the best-dressed man in Brody, which helped me get all the sex I wanted. Giving it up for the discipline of military school was asking a lot. Moses's father scared me off. I was torn with anger at my mother for getting pregnant, at the pressure from my peers to become a soldier and wear medals on my chest, and at the horrid stories of what military school would actually be like. Also, the thought of relocating with so many unknowns was not reassuring to me. I had a very difficult decision to make. I wanted to get as far away from Mother as I could. I missed Father, however, and wanted to see him again.

While I was in the midst of making this decision, Mendel Friedman was born on June 9, 1945. He was an embarrassment to me right from the beginning. Although I had my freedom, I was not independent. I earned neither my clothing nor my food. I saw that I could get those things in the army. A little brother certainly did not fit in with my plans.

My buddy Misha, who took over the Komsomol party, was very proud of my opportunity. He wished it were he who was going. When I was around him and his optimism, I made a pledge to go to the military school. Misha had a brother who was an officer, and Misha himself wanted to be an architect. Together, we would rebuild Mother Russia. Meanwhile, my mother registered me to go to Poland with her as family.

Mother was persistent. She made sure that I continued to hear terrible stories about military school. She knew I wanted to see Father again, and she worked that angle as much as possible. Mostly because of this, she got her wish.

On the day of our departure, we took our few bundles of possessions and went to the train station. There were about twenty families there. We all waited for the cattle cars to come. After we had been there about five hours, Misha appeared. He had come to say good-bye to a Polish girl, and when he spotted me, he turned red with anger. He came over and grabbed my arm very hard. He pulled me away from the group of people.

"You're a traitor to Mother Russia," he said. "Do you know what we do to traitors? We shoot them."

"I had no choice," I told him. "I'm a minor. Mother is forcing me to go."

"Why didn't you report her to the party? The party must come before your parents and your brothers."

"I'll come back," I told him. "I am just going to Poland to see my father. Afterwards, I'll come back."

Isaac came over to tell me the train was loading. "Let's go," he said.

I tried to hug Misha. He took a step back. I held out my hand to him, but he turned the other way. I felt bad for betraying my friend. For one day I did not talk to Mother at all.

The train trip from Brody to Gliwice in Silesia took about two weeks. It took so long because they used to uncouple our freight cars and leave us sitting for a couple days at a time before re-hooking us again to the locomotives. The locomotives were desperately needed to move Russian material out of German factories, which were being pilfered by the Russians. Tracks everywhere had been heavily damaged by the war. Freight cars were continually being added. My new kid brother was three months old and crying all the time. The Russian army would set up a kitchen and feed us like dogs.

I was rude and obnoxious to everybody. I was miserable and cold and going against my will. Even when I was a little boy I had wanted to be an officer, and now I had given up the chance. Mother was afraid I was going to jump the train and go back to Brody. I was happy to let her worry. But I was afraid that the Russians would not trust me anymore. My family was now in a different country, and my loyalty might be questioned. Maybe they would send me to Siberia as a traitor instead of to officers' school. So I endured the train ride.

It was a terrible experience. People were crowded into cars. My infant brother was constantly crying, and there were no bathrooms. If you had to urinate, you would push the door open and just do it. If you had to move your bowels, you either had to hold it in or foul your pants. When the train stopped, everyone would rush off, squat down, and do whatever they had to do. There was no such thing as modesty. We did not change our clothes. The cold weather combined with the other experiences made me feel as if we were back in hiding. Again, we were in a small space, with room to walk only over and around people. At night, we shared the light of a single lantern. The entire trip was hell, all the more so because I had grown accustomed to living a somewhat pampered lifestyle.

Then my dreams began. The setting was so clear—Mr. and Mrs. Symchuck's dwelling, about one thousand square feet for them and their two children, a horse, a cow, a sheep, two lambs, and us. The dwelling was divided—half for the family, and half for us captives in the barn. They had one enclosed room with a dirt floor. They cooked and ate and slept in this one room. The straw roof extended over the stable area—a high, inverted, V-shaped roof that created an attic for storage of hay and supplies. In one easterly corner was a haven for Jews, a haven carved out of the hay, just above the animals. The middle of the space offered the best chance to stand up. But you could never quite stand up. What a place it was! Our decor was straw and hay all around except for a wall of one-by-one boards. How real the dream becomes. There we are, working on a knot on a board until it pops out. From our hillside perch we can see out into the village. One of us is always looking through the hole, seeing people we once knew.

In one of my first dreams, I saw a small boy playing on our nearby ranch. I was consumed with jealousy and despair. Here I was in this hole, so hungry, dirty, and scared to speak out lest someone should hear me. There was always the fear somebody would spot us.

The dreams were so vivid and my rage so strong. I would need to scream out to test my vocal chords. In my dreams I would think that all this suffering was not worth it because we were going to die eventually at the hands of the Germans, or by starving in the barn. Why go through this agony day after day with no end in sight? I would dream about the frustration of always keeping these thoughts to myself.

So, as we rode, my thoughts went back to our captivity. Because I was so cramped on the train, I daydreamed of crawling over the Symchucks' bedroom to listen for news. At least then I could move. I relived the gripping fear I felt after I overheard the younger children crying to their parents that they should get rid of us.

A jolt of the boxcar would startle me out of my dream. I would look around and think it miraculous that we were still alive. I wondered if Father had reasoned ahead of time how wise it would be to have separate hiding places? If we had all been together at our place, surely the Symchucks would have killed us all. Or there would have been too many of us, and we all would have been caught and killed by the Germans or the Ukrainians. It was hard to make sense of it all. I was thinking a lot about some superior force planning everything. Father, as smart as he was, was only human. Then again, why should God allow things like pogroms and this train ride? If there were a loving God, how could He have allowed the murder of so many innocent people like my grandmother, my aunts and uncles, my cousins?

Even when the train stopped, we were not allowed to visit the towns or the villages. We had to sit on the train. We finally reached Gliwice, in Silesia. During the Potsdam Conference after the war, the victors Roosevelt, Churchill, and Stalin had reapportioned Central Europe. Stalin got the western Ukraine (which before the war was Poland), Latvia, Lithuania, and Estonia. Poland got lower Silesia, a German industrial area known for its coal mining.

We moved into a house owned by Germans. We had one room and a kitchen, where I shared a bed with Isaac. Mother, Mendel, and Sarah slept on a bed in another room. Within two weeks after we arrived in Gliwice, Father came home from the army and Sarah moved out. Our house in Gliwice was more like a duplex. In the other half lived a German woman with two daughters. One of these daughters, Hilda, was sixteen and very attractive. She could not speak any Polish nor I any German, but we were able to communicate in Yiddish, which had many German words. It was more than a month since I had had any sex.

Hilda showed interest in me and followed me around. She told me she had been raped by the Russians, who took their revenge upon the German women for what the Germans did to Russian women. As my desire for her grew, I did not think of her as a German. She was a girl and a very sexy one, and I was a man who had been without a woman for a long time.

We shared food and drank together. I felt compassion toward her. My desire to have her was intense, and I coaxed her into the kitchen one day to the bed I shared with Isaac. He pretended to be asleep.

"What about him?" she asked.

"He's a very sound sleeper," I told her.

I relished making love to her, not only because she satisfied my urge for sex but because she represented my triumph over the Germans. I felt that I was proving Hitler and Goebbels wrong, that I had fouled up their plan for a master race. Now, I was pouring my Jewish semen into a German girl, my first one. Still, my joy was muted. I felt powerful, but there was something flat about it, like soda without the fizz. This, along with Isaac pretending to be asleep beside us, made the whole act disappointing. I experienced no real satisfaction.

# The Survivors

I T WAS TIME TO BEGIN MEETING OTHER SUR-
vivors of the war. My cousin Pepe had also moved into the area. She
lived in a nearby town called Bytom. I bumped into her one afternoon at the local train station.

"I'd like you to meet a group of young Jewish people who live in a
commune," she said. "They earn a living making shoe polish, and perhaps they can be of some help to you." At the commune she introduced
me to a group of young Zionists, survivors like me, and to some Jewish
soldiers from Palestine, who were just visiting. These soldiers had been
part of a brigade in Africa, fighting along with the British. They wore
British uniforms without any rank, but with badges identifying them as
belonging to a Jewish brigade, just as I wore my Russian uniform without rank, though my reason was that I didn't have any civilian clothes to
wear at that time.

My first night at the commune, I listened to the soldiers tell stories
about Palestine. We sang Yiddish and Hebrew songs. I experienced an
intense feeling of belonging to a family, something I had lost because of
the war. I was ready to go to Palestine, which they had convinced me was

the Promised Land. I decided to join Hashomer Hatzeir, the Zionist group to which the members of this commune belonged. One of the historic leading members of Hashomer, Mordechai Anielewicz, had led the Warsaw Ghetto uprising. I had heard many stories about his courage, and he was someone I could admire. After all, he had died as a hero fighting the Nazis.

I had been deeply disappointed in how the Jews had reacted to the Nazis. Like so many other survivors, I believed that we had gone to the gas chambers like sheep. I often asked myself why we didn't take up arms and organize ourselves. Why had the rabbis seemed so passive, encouraging prayer rather than action to defend ourselves? Little did I understand that the Germans had taken away all our leaders and all our intelligentsia. Nor did I know that there had been pockets of armed Jewish resistance. Now I was with a group who vowed to take action, whose motto was "Never again."

I met Fruma on my second day at the commune. She was about sixteen but looked closer to twenty. She had survived one of the concentration camps in Poland. It was a small camp, but nevertheless thousands of Jews died there. The labor and the cruel conditions in these small camps achieved the same result as the gas chambers in the large extermination camps. I can't remember the name of this camp because there were so many in the Ukraine, Poland, and Germany. We tend to remember only the big camps, not the smaller ones, but the hell and torture in each were comparable.

Fruma survived because of a Ukrainian guard who took a liking to her, although he abused her in many ways. I had become accustomed to hearing such horror stories. Hers was just another. Now she was sleeping in a room with ten other boys and girls, and I managed to make love to her that second night. I didn't know what to expect from her. In Brody I had found sex to be fun-loving and playful. I still saw myself as a conqueror of women. I suppose I expected some kind of heavenly reward because she was my first Jewish girl, but all in all, we were both too anxious to really enjoy ourselves. Although very skinny, she felt heavy in my arms, as if the memories of the camps still numbed her body, and I felt sorry for her as we embraced each other.

Although I was enamored of the Hashomer, I was still too independent to give up my freedom. Besides I wanted to make money. My work as a shoe-polish salesman lasted a short time. Father had figured out a way for us to make some real money. We would buy clothing from the Germans who lived in that area. They needed the cash to buy sugar, salt, and coffee. Father and I would then travel by freight train to Krakow and sell the clothes on the open market. It was a two-day trip to Krakow, and we sat in straw on the floor.

Once, as we rode, Father became tired and dozed off. Near us, an attractive red-headed Polish woman lay on a blanket. I crawled in with her underneath the blanket, and we made love. As soon as I left her, her willingness to have sex with a total stranger worried me. I became scared to death that I might have picked up some disease.

Father started home early from the trip, leaving me to sell the clothes. Alone, I fretted more and more. I did not know the woman's name and she didn't know mine. We had spoken very few words to each other. She was simply another female who had fulfilled my lust. I had not cared at all about satisfying her. We had acted on base physical desire and did not think about the consequences. It was a good thing I had some selling to do, because it helped to keep my mind off the disease I was sure I had acquired.

I had learned from other guys that you could pick up gonorrhea or syphilis from casual sex. They told me that the symptoms of gonorrhea would show up in three days and that it was an easy infection to cure, but that syphilis was really bad. I concluded that there was no way I could have syphilis, that if I were to contract a sexually transmitted disease it would be the less severe gonorrhea. If I had to pay for treatment, I planned to tell Father I was robbed of a few thousand *zlotys* rather than confess I had spent the money for medical care. I had prepared myself for getting venereal disease, but something *else* happened instead.

On the return trip from Krakow to Gliwice, after I'd sold the clothes, my train collided with another train. Several people were killed, many injured. My life seemed full of chaos, one unexpected calamity after another. It was a pattern I was becoming used to. The Russians shot the Polish engineer because some of their soldiers had been killed in the accident. This was in January 1946, only seven months after the war had ended, and the Russians were the dominating force in Poland at the time. I came out of the train wreck relatively unscathed, with only a few bruises and a scratch on my head. But because of the accident, I arrived in Gliwice at about three o'clock in the morning.

Gliwice was not a safe place. Germans were still in the area. Poles were moving in and taking over possessions from the Germans by legal and illegal means. The middle of the night was the most dangerous time. Bandits would hold you up and take everything you had. Those guys did not care if you were a Pole or a German. We used to protect ourselves and our money by putting our valuables in our boots. I was carrying two empty suitcases and a rucksack on my back that night, when I was stopped by a couple of Polish bandits.

"Where are you going?" they demanded.

"I am being repatriated from Russia," I said. "I was delayed because of a train wreck."

"What's your address?" they said.

I told them.

They pointed me in the direction of my house and let me go.

DURING MY STAY in Gliwice, I was mostly irresponsible. When my buddies and I would get onto a streetcar and see Germans sitting in the seats that we wanted, we would kick them out of their seats and take them for ourselves. It was easy to pick on Germans because the Polish government made them wear white armbands for quick identification. Most of the German men were in either prison or detention camps, so Germans on the bus tended to be women or older men.

Looking back, I am not proud of what we did, but at the time, it seemed perfectly all right to make life miserable for these Germans. Once, I saw a German on a bicycle.

"Get off," I told him.

He hardly protested. I took the bicycle and rode away. At the time, it seemed like the very least I was entitled to. My friends and I shared the feeling that we were living for each day. In that sense, it was still like the war years — nothing mattered except the moment.

It's not surprising that my father and I were at odds much of the time. My attitude angered him, and he seemed always to be chiding me. I was in no mood to be continually lectured. After all, I had made it through some tough times, as had he, and the girls were crazy about me.

Life was serious business for Father. For me, my business was not limited to selling clothes but included activities my father didn't approve of. I was confident and selfish, living from moment to moment to satisfy my own pleasures.

In Katowic, I joined a Jewish theater group as a tap dancer. As my costume for each performance, I wore striped pants, a black frock coat, and a black silk top hat. My dancing was well received, but owing to my other activities and my travel, I had to give up my life in the theater after only four weeks.

BECAUSE WE COULDN'T get along, Father and I split up as business partners. I was happy to be on my own. In Gliwice, people gathered in a huge public square to swap and sell clothes. I soon made a place for myself in this bazaar. You were supposed to have a permit, as everyone was supposed to be accounted for. The Polish government wanted to make sure no one was just loafing around. In my usual cocky manner, I ignored such details. I had a man's jacket to sell and considered myself as much a merchant as the next guy. The police suddenly surrounded me, and I was trapped without an escape route. They arrested me and put me in jail with a bunch of cutthroat criminals. Although I pretended not to be afraid, I was scared to death.

My fellow prisoners asked me for cigarettes, and I passed them out willingly. Meanwhile, they told me awful stories of what they had to do at night, like reaching into toilet buckets while blindfolded. The game was called "pick-a-cucumber." These were toilet buckets, however, not pickle barrels, and they were full of shit, not cucumbers.

These stories left me paralyzed with fear. Eight of us were packed into one cell, and the stench was terrible. A small window up on the wall represented the only ray of hope. It faced the street, offering a narrow glimpse onto the sidewalk and the feet of passing pedestrians. I moved near it to collect my wits, and I prayed to God as hard as I could. Mr. Big Shot was on his own all right. No one knew where I was. I prayed hard because I didn't know what else to do. As I stood by the window, quivering, I looked up and saw the boots of Pepe's husband Joseph walking by. I was sure they were Joseph's boots — his were very new and had been custom-made to look like riding boots.

"Joseph!" I yelled.

He heard me, but he couldn't figure out where the noise was coming from.

"Joseph! Joseph!" I yelled.

He bent down finally and saw me. He went to the police station and paid them to let me out. It was a miracle that he saw me at all.

After the jail episode, I accompanied him to his home. He was planning on a move to another city, and he wanted me to keep Pepe company while he scouted it out. He left the next day, and I was to stay that night until he returned.

Pepe and I were good friends. She was really like a sister. Joseph had been married before and had lost his wife and two children during the war. He was fifteen years older than Pepe, and she liked having someone nearer her age to talk with. That night we talked long into the wee hours of the morning. She told me that Joseph seemed distant at times. I told her how unhappy I was and asked if she thought I should go back to Russia.

"Maybe," she said. "You should be happy."

I was getting sleepy sitting on the couch.

"Why don't we share my large bed in my bedroom?" she asked. "We'll be more comfortable there."

We continued talking in her bedroom, late into the night.

"You should consider going to Palestine," she said. "After all, now you're a member of the Hashomer."

I didn't reply to this suggestion. I was embarrassed to admit that I had joined the Hashomer group in part because they were the most popular and active Jewish group in Katowitz and had more women than men members.

Eventually, our intimate conversation led to intimate lovemaking, and we finally fell asleep. I was never invited to stay at her house again. She must have told Joseph.

Right after the Kelce pogrom in June of 1946, Pepe and Joseph left Poland for Palestine, but they first spent some time in Italy in a displaced-persons camp. They arrived illegally in Palestine at the end of 1947 or the beginning of 1948. Pepe gave birth to a daughter. Tragically, Pepe died of tuberculosis when her daughter was not even two years old.

IN FEBRUARY 1946, we got ready to move to Waldenburg, which was the German name for a town the Poles called Walbrzych.

Father paid a Russian man a bottle of vodka to help us find a place to live. This fellow found a house some Germans were living in, and he kicked them out for us. We were then free to move in.

This was our last home in Poland. Waldenburg was near the Czecho-slovakian border, and Jews were often leaving from there for somewhere else. Italy was a popular destination, and so was Palestine. Maybe this is why we ended up in Waldenburg. Perhaps Father was putting in motion a plan to leave Poland by moving us to such a town.

The house was big. My parents rented the upstairs to three broth-ers. One them, Uri, was about six years older than I, and he became my business partner. Most factories were still shut down from the war. The Germans, who now lived in territory annexed by Poland, were eager to trade their clothing for local currency to buy butter, bread, milk, and other necessities. We would go to the villages and buy clothing from the Germans at a low price and sell it on the open market in Krakow. The goods moved so fast that we knew we were on to something big.

We hired a couple of local German women, Monika and Grethe, to promote our business and help us with the transactions. They were happy to work for coffee, sugar, and flour. In addition, they enjoyed mak-ing love to us. We developed a simple routine. We would arrive in the village very early in the morning and have a big breakfast and then make love to Monika and Grethe. Then Uri and I would sleep while the women went out to the villagers. "The Jews are here," they would say. "They want to buy your goods."

By noon we joined the gathering at a local farmhouse and traded coffee, salami, sugar—all very scarce commodities—in exchange for clothing. Because these villagers were hungry, they were eager to ex-change their material possessions for food, or for money that would help them buy food. Shoes, suits, sweaters were pulled from hiding places.

It was easy for me in my mind's eye to see these villagers digging in some secret place for their valuable articles. Our family and friends— for that matter everyone I knew in our home village—had hidden pos-sessions during the war. Nevertheless, sympathy was the furthest thing from my mind. I was obsessed with the laws of supply and demand.

Still, we tried not to take advantage of the situation. We developed a reputation for honesty because we had the good sense to be reason-able. We were relaxed because we knew we could sell the unsold goods at a profit in Waldenburg. When we were finished, all we had to do was load up our bicycles and go back to the city.

On a day when Uri left early, the police stopped me while I was peddling my bicycle and demanded to see a working permit.

"What are you doing here?" they asked.

"I just bought some things," I told them.

"Do you have a permit?"

"No," I told them. "I don't have a permit."

They arrested me and put me into a cellar with rotten potatoes. They gave me nothing to eat and took all my money and goods away. When it got dark, I started banging on the gate to the cell.

"You already have my money. It's getting dark," I screamed. "Give me some food. I'm hungry."

I began to wonder how long I was going to be in there and what they were going to do to me. Just then, someone came into the police station. He turned out to be a local Jew who had taken over a large German farm. I had no idea who he was, but I started making as much noise as I could.

"I'm a Jew! Let the Jew out!" I screamed.

Something inside me just told me to raise a ruckus, and I hollered and carried on. The visitor heard me and demanded to know what was going on.

"We've picked up some Yid, a peddler without a permit," the policeman said. The farmer asked to talk to me. We never saw each other before or after that, but he managed to talk the police into releasing me.

"Don't you ever come back to this village," one of the policemen said. And you can bet I never did.

SOPHIE WAS A nineteen-year-old village girl who helped me buy merchandise from her people. I met her when my partner Uri hired her as a live-in housekeeper and cook for the three brothers living above us. Naturally, I got to know her and learned her story.

Her grandmother had raised her and always protected her. When the Russians came, they were afraid, because the Russian soldiers were infamous rapists, so Sophie's grandmother prepared a hiding place in a field cellar where they kept potatoes from freezing in winter and spoiling from the heat in summer. Sophie spent at least two weeks down there. The cellar was very dark, and afterwards she had a hard time getting used to the daylight.

When I found out Sophie was a virgin, I couldn't believe it. I did not think the Russians had left untouched any German woman between the ages of eight and eighty! Since she was important to my business, I took things very slow with Sophie. It took me five trips of courting before I cornered her. I was thankful to her grandmother for saving this virgin for me. That she was a German and a virgin was crucial, for now I would really be getting even for what Germans had done to Jewish women.

Father and I rejoined forces out of necessity, trading currency and goods for clothing and then selling the clothes in Krakow. We would ride a couple of passenger trains overflowing with people all the way from Waldenburg to Krakow, a total of thirty-six hours. Father wore a Polish army uniform, and I wore a Russian one. He would jump onto the train before me, get into the bathroom, and open the window. I would hand him our merchandise from the platform and then climb through the window before the train started moving. We locked ourselves in the restroom for the first twelve-hour segment of the trip. People would beat on the door, but we would not let them in.

In Breslau, partway to Krakow, we would get off the train because the bridge on the Oder River was destroyed. We had to switch trains, but first there was a five-mile walk because the track was not yet repaired from the war. German girls would come to the Breslau train station with little wagons. We put our baggage on the wagons, and they would pull everything to the next station. We boarded the train again on the other side of the river in Breslau, repeating our routine of locking ourselves in the bathroom. This final part of the trip, from Breslau to Krakow, took twenty-four hours. Occasionally we had to pay off the conductor.

The last time Father and I traveled together in this fashion, we arrived in Krakow about 5 p.m. and checked into a run-down hotel. Our room had no toilet or bathtub, just a bed and a place to wash your face. Since I was still a member of Hashomer, I told my father I was going to eat at their commune in Krakow, where I could take a bath. Most of the members living there were young survivors of the Holocaust, from the ages of sixteen to thirty, and most of them were waiting to go to Palestine. When I got to the commune, I met an attractive woman in her mid-twenties. She seemed eager to have sex, and I gladly obliged her.

By the time I got back to the hotel, it was after three in the morning. I had to waken Father because I had no key. He yelled and called me all kinds of nasty names. Then he smacked my face.

"You idiot," he said. "When are you going to stop whoring around? You'll get venereal disease and die from it."

"I can no longer put up with your tirades," I answered back. "Let's split up and go into business on our own."

"Fine," he said. "Take the next load of merchandise to Krakow by yourself. Let's see how you make it, out on your own."

Determined to do well, I wore two or three of the suits, then wrapped a whole cloth around me and put my Russian overcoat over the top. What a sight I must have been! I carried two to four suitcases and a rucksack on my back. Then came the task of trying to ride the train. It was jammed. I decided to put all the baggage on the roof of the train and ride up there myself, holding onto the railing all the way to Wroclaw. It was awkward, but I managed to tie down both myself and the luggage.

Quickly I developed strategies for surviving on all these business trips. In the Breslau train station, on the way to Krakow, I would stand next to the Russian soldiers in my Russian uniform. They would clear the train car of civilians and take the car over for themselves. The soldiers would ask me what I was up to with all my gear, and I would tell them I was on my way back to Russia. As I spoke Polish, I could invite the Polish women onto the train, and this would make the soldiers happy. Upon arriving in Krakow, I stayed at the Hashomer commune. In the daytime, I conducted my business and at night returned to the commune, where seven out of ten members were women. So I always had a sleeping partner. There was never any romance involved, just unmitigated sexual gratification. We all still felt as if we had no idea what tomorrow might bring.

One of my frequent partners was a woman about six years older than I. She was great in bed and very shrewd. After one of our lovemaking sessions, she told me she might be pregnant with my child. I felt my world suddenly darken. "You can't be pregnant," I told her. "Not if you don't want a child."

She knew of a doctor who would take care of the problem, but she told me it would cost me some money. I agreed to pay for an abortion.

I never stayed in that commune again, nor did I ever see her again. Later, I discovered from one of my friends that she had lied to me. I wasn't too upset, however, because I realized her story was just what I needed. Sex was there for the taking, like fruit during harvest, and I never dreamed it could spoil. I was much more careful in the future. I didn't curtail my sexual escapades, but I protected myself. Often I would not even share my real name with my partner.

ON ONE OCCASION Father and I happened to be at the train station together. I was walking ahead of him, with enough material draped around me for a suit, a suit underneath the material, and my Russian army overcoat on top of everything. I carried two suitcases and a rucksack on my back. Father was following me with two more suitcases. The police spotted me and asked to see my papers. Father saw what was happening and immediately turned back and took his suitcases home. We lived near the station, and he returned in a short time to keep an eye on me. While the police talked to me, Father grabbed my two suitcases and took them home.

"You crooks!" I said to the police. "What have you done with my bags?"

"It was the old man who was following you," one of them said.

"What old man?" I yelled. "You crooks stole my suitcases."

"Okay, you smart son of a bitch, let's go to the police station."

We walked there slowly. "What will you give us to set you free?" one of them asked.

"How much do you want?" I asked.

"About four bottles of vodka," he said.

"Why the hell should I pay you anything?" I replied.

For some reason they decided to turn around and go back to the train station to try and catch the old man who had taken the suitcases. When we returned there, the police got an emergency call and turned me over to the railroad police, and they in turn dragged me to their holding room, which was hotter than hell.

"I know that you have gold on you," the senior officer among them said. "We've been ordered to stop the flow of gold out of the country."

"What do you mean?" I said. "I have no gold. Why are you picking on me? I have done nothing wrong."

Another policeman came into this hot room. He noticed that I was sweating heavily.

"I bet he has gold on him," he said.

"You're just making up stories," I shouted back.

"Take off your clothes," one of them said. "We'll find out real fast."

I peeled off one layer, then another, then another. They looked at me, confused for a second, and then exclaimed, pointing to the pile of clothing.

"This is gold! You're a smuggler." They were referring to my clothing business.

Now they handcuffed me and walked toward the police station. My mother, who had been looking for me, found us and whispered to me in Yiddish, "Pay them off, whatever they are asking."

But I was angry and had no intention of giving them anything. Soon I was in jail, wondering why I hadn't paid them off.

"How stupid you are," I thought. "Why didn't you listen to your mother? You could have been out and on your way to Krakow." I sat there behind black iron bars. I felt the deadly fear that I had felt before, both in jails and when hiding from the Nazis. This fear began to choke me. I knew these cops didn't like Jews, and I didn't know what was going to happen to me.

But, like the biblical Joseph in the dungeon, I had a change of luck. The two city policemen who had originally arrested me came to claim me, and this set off an argument between them and the railroad police. A big argument followed about who had jurisdiction over me. The city police claimed they had arrested me first, and the railroad police claimed that I was going to use the railroad for black-marketing. Both claims, of course, were true.

The city policemen won the argument. You can't imagine how happy I was to be out of the railroad police jail. They had a reputation for being the worst bastards. The regular policemen marched me straight to their station.

"This time," one of them said, "we're going to keep you in our jail."

"If you put me in jail," I said, "I'm going to squeal on you because you asked me for a bribe when you first arrested me, and I wouldn't pay. I'll make you an offer — enough money for a bottle of vodka for my release, or I squeal." They took the money.

After they released me, I sat down in the train station to think about all the misery that had come my way for being cocky. The trains were no longer running, and I decided to go home.

My penitence didn't last long. All in all, I was proud of how I had escaped jail. Moreover, in the end I didn't fork over much money for my release. I confidently told my parents the whole story.

"You idiot," Father said. "You might have been in that jail for a year. You're a hothead. You don't even know how much danger you were in. Maybe you belong in jail if you're going to be so reckless. You had your mother worried sick."

"I'm sorry," I said.

"No, you're not," he said. "Listen to yourself. You were just bragging."

"No, I wasn't."

"Okay, big shot," he said. "From now on, no more freeloading. You're to pay for room and board."

He reached for his wallet, took my share of rent and food money, and threw the bills on the floor.

"There," he said. "That's yours. And we're through as partners. I don't want to work with such a cocky imbecile, someone who'd risk everything for a few smart remarks."

Years later, after I had my own children in America, I would come to appreciate my father. When I was being a rebellious young jerk, he pushed me to be independent and responsible. I attribute much of my success today to him. Of course, I was angry and hurt that night, but even then, as I sat there chastened by him, I knew deep inside that he was right.

I resumed buying and selling clothing on my own. Strangely enough, I began to feel sorry for the Germans because it was now they who were so helpless. Mostly I saw only women, children, and very old people. The German men in 1946 were withering in labor camps or were still prisoners of war in Poland or Russia. The Poles had taken over German farms, with the German women and children working under them. I reflected on my image of the Germans just four years ago. When they walked, they sounded like ten times their number and looked as if they were ten feet tall. Our fear of them was so great. We would hear them two miles away, and it would seem as if they were right next door. They were boisterous and proud in their uniforms. I remember hoping that when we were liberated, all the Germans would be put in cages and taken to different cities like animals. We would show the world: here were the monsters and the murderers of innocent people.

Now, in 1946, I began to feel sorry for these German women and children because their lives were terrible. I could see their suffering, and I discovered some new part of being human. Thank God most humans are forgiving. My need for revenge was no longer there. To be honest, I didn't go out of my way to make their lives easier, but I did try to be fair in my business dealings.

# Confusion
# for My
# People

𐎀

AN YOU IMAGINE SIX MILLION JEWS LETTING
themselves get killed? To this day, it angers me that this could
happen, that God could allow it. I can still see a rabbi caught
by the Germans. They pulled off his beard. Pieces of his skin were attached to the hairs the Nazis pulled out. I and my fellow Jews just stood
there and watched. Not one person lifted a finger to intervene. I cried
and the others cried, but we should have fought back. In part, we were
paralyzed by disbelief in what was happening all around us. But that is
no excuse.

Only later did I discover that we were not all so passive.

When we arrived in Gliwice in 1945 and heard of the Warsaw
Ghetto uprising, I was so proud. I became a great admirer of Mordechai
Anielewicz, a young leader of the uprising who had lost his life fighting
the Nazis. The Germans had made us believe the Jews were helpless.
When I learned that during the uprising we fought back with guns, I was
a little less ashamed.

The Germans did a skillful job of hiding the fact that Jews fought
with partisans all over Europe, using guerrilla tactics in and out of

ghettos. The Nazis' control of information prevented more resistance. I came to realize later that Jews fought back in many places, by breaking out of Sobibor and by rioting at Treblinka and Auschwitz. Moreover, I didn't know then how cruel some of the Poles had been to Jewish partisans who joined the underground and were then killed by the very Poles they were fighting to help. My own father's outsmarting of the Germans was a great act of resistance. His hiring a teacher so we wouldn't fall behind in our learning was another act of defiance. But I am still left with the puzzle of how so many of my people let the Germans march them off to the death camps.

The Germans organized the murder of the Jews. But it was the Poles, Ukrainians, Russians, Hungarians, Romanians, Latvians, Estonians, French, Italians, Czechs, and even the officials of the Vatican who all went along in a shocking manner. The only people in all of Europe who took it upon themselves to save Jews were the Danes and in some ways the Bulgarians. Why did only one nation in the world stand up to the atrocities? And where was America? Why was America so quiet?

Perhaps someday historians will come up with an answer. I still wonder if it didn't have something to do with Christians thinking that the Jews murdered Jesus Christ. As a boy, I was aware that Polish schools taught that Jews killed Christ. What better reason could be given to hate Jews? It was never mentioned that Jesus was himself a Jew. And as I found myself feeling sorry for destitute Germans soon after the war had ended, it seemed impossible that for hundreds of years people could be urged to hate. At least one good thing came out of this war. The Christian religions no longer teach that Jews killed Jesus.

To this day, no one has come close to explaining how God could have let such a disaster happen to His chosen people. Today I have mixed emotions when I speak of God. If He is a loving God, how could He have allowed anything like the Holocaust to happen? If it wasn't for some of the miracles that happened to my family and me, my faith in God would be nil. But I believed that God watched over us so that we could survive. Why He picked us, I don't know. I'm sure there were many righteous people among us. Father was charitable. He gave to the sick and downtrodden, to the rabbi and to the shul, to the beggars who knocked on our door. If it happened to be late on a Friday afternoon, my father would invite these poor people to spend the Sabbath with us. I remember that some of these unlucky people would tell great stories after supper. They seemed to me to be very intelligent, and I could not understand why they were poor. But the rabbis who were killed, one after another, were good men of God. My grandmother Klara was a fine woman, but the Germans set fire to her house with her still in it.

HERE I AM AGAIN, trying to make sense of something that will never make any real sense. At the time, such questions might have eaten me up if not for my constant pursuit of selfish pleasure. Had I brooded over what happened to my family, it would have killed me. Making love to women became an outlet for my frustration. Who knows? Perhaps my childish anger at Mother for giving birth to Mendel in 1945 and my subsequent jealousy of the baby played into my insatiable desire to conquer women. But I also craved being loved. As a child, I had a nanny who catered to my needs, and before the war I was pampered by my mother. I did not have the luxury to be a teenager, to move toward thoughtfulness. At sixteen, I became a man, and at seventeen, I was independent and my own boss. My mother had a baby to take care of.

Through it all, I seem to have been endowed with an ability to adapt. For a short time I might feel uncomfortable, but I usually convinced myself that things would turn out all right. If I needed to act like a monkey, then I would become a monkey if the occasion called for it.

When I think about those years immediately after the war, I am disturbed that I didn't keep in touch with many of the first people I came to know. Where are they now? Why didn't I take the time to keep track of the orphaned brother and sister from Pitkamien—the first Jews we met and lived with briefly after the war? Then we met another brother and sister when we went to Pitchayew. I saw a resemblance to our family in each of these survivors, but I lost track even of Uri and his brothers. We were happy to see other Jewish survivors, but in many ways we were shortsighted, still thinking only of our own needs and how to survive. Perhaps others felt differently. But I felt as if that part of us that was for others was wrung out by the war. I was still in a daze, like a robot with no plans for the future. I was supposed to be dead, but here I was alive, living on instincts. I had programmed myself to survive, and to seek pleasure wherever possible.

Why had I survived and not my relatives? I kept my emotional distance from everyone so as to avoid losing anyone ever again. As a result of Father's teachings and my own experiences, I trusted only myself. I was eighteen years old. Other survivors my age felt similarly. We all seemed to be living for the day.

# Fleeing
Poland

I N 1946, A POGROM ERUPTED IN POLAND. WITH
no apparent provocation, young hoodlums in Kelce killed Jews and
looted their homes. By the time the police arrived, over forty Jews
were dead and more than twice that many were injured. News of this
pogrom spread like a plague through the Jewish survivors in Poland.
I couldn't believe that after so many Jews had been murdered in the
war, the Poles still felt animosity toward those few who had survived.
I would have thought that their hatred had abated.

The few Jews who still lived in Poland moved in droves to a safer
place. These included many Jews who had emigrated to Poland from labor camps in Russia. In Waldenburg, we were only fifty kilometers or so
from the Czech border. After the Kelce pogrom, we were sure we could
never be safe in Poland again.

Where would we go? Father contacted a man who could take us
across the border to Czechoslovakia. This would be a first step. Most of
the Jews in this part of Europe were landing in a displaced persons camp
(D.P. camp) in Austria and resettling from there. Sooner or later, those
in such camps would emigrate to Palestine. We, too, dreamed of going

to Palestine, where we would taste true freedom. In October 1946 we got rid of whatever we could sell or trade. We could take with us only what we could carry, and our guide made it clear that we were each limited to a small backpack.

At dawn, we got onto a train, not all at once but a few at a time. The journey was to another village even closer to the border, where our guide was waiting for us. He was a man about twenty-five years old. His name was Mordechai, but I called him "Heiss," the German word for cocky. He did not look cocky—he was thin and wore the clothes of a beggar—but he seemed in control, confident. Heiss was now in charge of our group.

We arrived in a small village three kilometers from the border. I am sure the Polish government knew of our intentions, but Heiss had bribed the local authorities. We were going to cross the border at night and on foot, illegally. Nothing was going to stop us from leaving. We were in all maybe twenty or thirty people.

Heiss told us to hide our money. We had mostly American dollars and gold coins. He knew that the obvious places where people hid money— shoes or socks—would not be effective. He recommended my father's method—rolling money into a condom and sticking it up the rectum. Now, looking back on that moment, I can feel the suspense and apprehension, but at the time, after everything else, it was just another thing we had to do in order to survive. I had five twenty-dollar bills rolled up in a condom that belonged to me. I assumed my father was carrying much more money than I. He did not tell me how much he had, because he still felt I could not be trusted.

Finally, the night came when we were to cross the border and leave Poland forever. The border policemen went through our possessions, which consisted only of clothing. Apparently the officials did not think we had any money, because they did not inspect us. We left the border and, just like that, Poland was behind us. In retrospect, I can only surmise that the Polish government acquiesced to Russian pressure to let us leave Poland. It was assumed that we would make our way to Palestine, where we would confront the British, an outcome the Russians supported.

Nobody felt very different, however, upon leaving Poland. It seemed as if nothing had changed in our wretched lives. Here we were, fleeing our homes like desperadoes, cold cash stuck up our assholes. Since our liberation by the Russians in 1945, we had moved from town to town in order to survive inside "liberated" Poland. We were still Jews and we were not safe in our fatherland. When daylight came, I looked back to Poland, feeling sad and empty inside.

Heiss sensed our anxiety. He got us into a circle as we waited for the Czech train and started talking about Palestine, our real homeland, where we could go and no one could kick us out. To be in the majority had great appeal to me. His words put Zionist fire in my heart again. At this dark time his hope was like balm to my soul, and I could clearly visualize us in the land of Palestine.

We were still afraid, however, and I still had the money up my rectum. Whenever I moved my bowels, I removed the money and then put it back when I had finished. Soon, we boarded another crowded train, this time to Bratislava. Once we got on the train, we thought it would be safe to pull the money out. Mine got stuck. I saw the devil, I tell you, trying to get that condom out. I needed the three days we had in the transit camp to recover from the ordeal.

A transit camp was set up in Bratislava for Jews who had to leave Poland. These camps were established by the Jewish underground with money from American Jews. Then we went to Austria, where our first stop was the Rothschild D.P. camp supported by the United Nations Relief Fund. Here we would be processed and our fate determined. Vienna, like Austria itself, was divided into four zones: Russian, British, American, and French. The Rothschild Hospital, which was used to house us temporarily, was in the American zone of Vienna. It took the Jewish agencies about one week to make arrangements for us to be housed in Enns, which was also in the American zone.

To get to Enns, however, we had to take the train from the Russian zone in Vienna and travel through the Russian zone of Austria, an area called lower Austria. The train ride took four to six hours. We were warned by a man in the camp, who specialized in getting people out of the Russian sector, to be especially careful during this train crossing. We had to get rid of any papers that had contained Russian or Polish writing. We destroyed all documents with photos taken when we lived in Poland or Russia. We also had to avoid speaking Polish or Russian. We would pretend to be Greeks trying to make our way home. By having us destroy all traces of our past, the Jewish Agency made it impossible for us ever to go back to Poland or Russia. We didn't know this; we simply acted out of fear of the Russian inspectors. To this day, however, I regret shredding our pasts — especially the family photos.

We had gotten rid of all incriminating pictures or documents. We thought we had taken care of everything. Still, one of our little girls of about age six saw a Russian soldier approaching and blurted out, "Look, here comes a *krasnoarmeiets!*" which means "Red Army soldier" in Russian. Most everyone just froze, thinking this was the end. But fortunately, either he didn't hear her or didn't want to hear her, because he paid no attention. The train pulled out of the Soviet sector of Vienna and headed toward the Enns River and a crossing to the American sector.

In Enns, they had made an old German army camp into the first stop for refugees arriving from Vienna. These were Jews escaping from Russia, Poland, Romania, Hungary, and Czechoslovakia. They arrived at Enns in all kinds of desperate ways. Enns was originally to be a transient camp, just a stopover on the way to the D.P. camps, but by the time we arrived most of the D.P. camps were already full, especially in Italy, because the British were doing such a good job of keeping the Jews out of Palestine.

Some of the refugees got administration jobs in the Enns camp, but most of us did not have any jobs. We ate in a communal dining hall. The camp was officially called "Green Shelter Lager 106 Enns," and the building in which refugees were housed was a huge, three-storey, L-shaped structure. In the beginning, there was a lot of boredom, but after a while, some of the people got used to this kind of life and others decided to go back to Poland. Many people who had arrived as singles got married, and then, later, children were born in camp. Those who stayed made out the best way they could. Some purchased hot plates so they could prepare their own meals. Schools were set up for the children. Most of us were waiting for the order to pack for Palestine.

The camp itself was on the Enns River, which divided the American zone from the Russian zone. One of the strange things I remember was swimming in this river, which was only twenty feet wide. The Russians were just across from us. We would yell insults at them, happy because they couldn't send us to Siberia. This still stands out in my mind because it was so adolescent, so unlike anything I had been able to do as a teenager up to that point.

The camp at Enns grew to about fifteen hundred people. The governments still had no idea how to settle the refugee problem, and our life in the barracks became semipermanent. We had one large room for the five of us and we slept in bunks. The camp was maintained by the Jewish police and the U.S. Army, although the United Nations supplied the food. There were other large camps of refugees around, plus the military garrisons. There was an American garrison six kilometers away and another thirty kilometers distant. I would soon learn that these outposts were to be the key to my next business opportunities.

# The Black
# Market

I BECAME VERY INDEPENDENT. IMMEDIATELY, I
was out buying and selling, making a lot of money and discover-
ing the nightclubs of Linz and Salzburg. The proprietors called me
Mr. Friedman because I was such a big shot with spending money. I also
knew by then that if you acted fearless and sure of yourself at all times,
you could do as you pleased.

My brashness came in handy in my encounters with the Austrians,
who looked upon us as unwelcome outsiders. I became a good fighter by
getting in the first solid punch, then ducking the comeback or having an
outsider break up the fight. If there was a problem, I would grab the other
guy and start punching him first. My strategy was to grab the lapels or
the front of my opponent's clothing and let him have the top of my head
under his chin as I yanked him hard toward me. This would cause a guy
to almost pass out or bite his tongue, or might loosen his teeth. I became
a street fighter. There was no such thing as a clean fight. My clothes
would get torn, but I had the respect of the other guys. The word was
out: "Don't screw around with Heniek." I was glad others wanted to ac-
company me on evening forays, because I did fear being jumped by a
gang seeking revenge.

I protected my younger brother Isaac. The war had stunted his growth, he was very small for his age and still was not growing at all. Nevertheless, he was well on his way to being a genius in school. He was also a passionate Zionist and actor, appearing in several school plays. I was very proud of him. Whenever he needed to buy something, I would give him the money. Although we were only six years apart, it seemed more like ten years.

Mother was always caring for the baby, Mendel, and I had very little to do with them.

MY FIRST BUSINESS venture while living in the compound involved selling sugar. I met a guy in a bar who said he could sell me some sugar. He must have stolen it, because sugar was a ration card item and in short supply. It was also very expensive on the black market, but he quoted me a low price. Unfortunately, I was out of cash from a recent spending spree. I went to my father for a loan.

"Where is all your money, big shot?" he asked.

"I've spent it," I told him.

"Too bad," he said.

At the time, I had a gold stopwatch worth fifty dollars and also a signet ring with my initials on it that was worth about twenty dollars. I recruited a partner, Johann, who could throw in a little money, and we went to the guy to work out a deal. We gave him my watch and ring, plus my partner's money as a deposit, and agreed to pay him off the next day. I can't remember whether the sack of sugar weighed fifty or a hundred kilos, but we spent the night putting it into small packs.

Then we hit the road, making two trips from Enns to Linz in one day. We made a good profit. The next day we were able to pay up and order much more sugar, and I took on a third partner as well. His name was Petru, and he was a survivor of Buchenwald concentration camp. He had lost his toes on both feet due to frostbite and wore special shoes. Petru was totally alone in the world — all his family had perished in the camps. We struck up a good partnership because we were hungry to make money. Our goal was to make as much as possible during the day and then to spend it fast in the clubs at night.

The key to expanding our business became the American garrison at Enns. We discovered a source for French cognac in Innsbruck and sold it for a huge profit to the GIs who guarded the border on the Enns River against the Russians. We then got into a trading scam with U.S. script money that was issued to American military personnel. The GIs needed script to purchase items at the base, and they were happy to trade dollars sent from home. Nine hundred U.S. dollars were worth about a thousand dollars of script. We in turn were happy to have the dollars, which we could use to purchase items cheaply on the black market and resell at a profit.

We began to trade in gold and jewelry, which we bought on the black market from the Austrians. We also discovered a large supply of stolen blankets in our camp, which were offered to us at a bargain price. We were able at not much risk to sell them quickly on the black market. Everywhere we looked, there was a new way to make money.

Johann was leaving for Germany, so I picked up another partner. His name was Issie. He was from Poland, and he and his father and his two sisters lived about one hundred kilometers from us, but we didn't know them before the war. They were survivors — one look at Issie and you knew not to mess with him. He was not a woman chaser because he was in love with an Austrian woman and was living with her. In fact, he wanted to marry her, but his father objected vigorously, and so he didn't. Like all my partners, Issie was five or six years older than I.

We were working a lot at a D.P. camp called Bindermichel, in Linz, where there was a great demand for our wares. While we were there, we loaded up on American cigarettes. We would sell them to the Austrians. The same thing with coffee. We had big mark-ups on just about everything.

We would buy a carton of cigarettes for 70 cents, then sell it for $1.50 to $2.00 to Austrians. Then we would buy a bottle of cognac for $2.00 and sell it to GI's for maybe $6.00 to $8.00. We had regular customers who did our advertising for us. The same guys would come to us and exchange their script for Austrian shillings.

THE NEARBY TOWN OF Enns had only one movie theater, and there was always a long line to see the one show of the evening. By the time the people in our camp finished dinner in the communal dining room, they would be the last in line. Too often, they were turned away as the tickets were sold out. We decided to ask the management to sell us a block of tickets so we could sell them in advance to the camp people. The owner refused.

One night about twelve of us went to the theater. As usual, there was a big line, and as we waited at the end of it, our patience gave out. When the door opened, we sauntered to the front of the line. A policeman was standing with his foot between the doors, blocking our way.

"Get back at the end of the line," he said.

"I'm right here and I want to get in," I shot back.

"No," he said. "you have to go back in line."

I lifted my knee and hit him between the legs. A fight broke out. Before too long, a busload of policemen came and the twelve of us were arrested. We were charged with hitting a policeman. I was very angry and wished that I were armed. I thought of the Stern Group, organized to fight the British in Palestine and to recruit and coerce Jewish survivors in Europe to emigrate to Israel. They were beginning to become known for terrorist activities against the British after blowing up the British Embassy in Vienna. I told the police that I had to defend myself against the cop at that theater, and that if they continued to detain us I would get the Stern Group to blow up their police station. I completely bluffed my way out of the situation. We were released and warned not to start any more problems. By the way, we never again had to worry about getting blocks of tickets to the theater. The very mention of the Stern Group was enough to send shudders up the owner's spine.

THERE WAS A meat shortage in Austria at the time and we seized the opportunity. I met a guy named Bernie whose father had been a butcher. We joined up with a fellow named Aaron, who was eighteen years older than I, and Issie, my previous partner.

Aaron, who came from a large, impoverished Jewish family, had been a communist before the war. When the Russians moved into his city in 1939, however, he became disillusioned and spoke out against the communists. He and his family were sent to Siberia to cut wood, which took all the rest of the communist doctrine out of Aaron. Bernie had survived by hiding in the forest with his father and a brother. One month before liberation, his father gave himself up to save his sons. There hadn't been enough food; they were living off roots the last few months. More-over, the father, who had a chronic cough, didn't want to give away the hiding place of his children.

Issie and I specialized in rationed products and in money exchanges. We constantly had to shift from one commodity to another as our sup-ply ran out. Aaron and Bernie had many contacts among the Austrians and Jews in camp. It seemed natural to pool our resources in order to get some meat into the camp. Meat was rationed to the Austrians, but the refugees in the camp could not get a ration card for it. Outside the camp, the price of meat was too high on the black market.

We found a farmer who agreed to sell us a cow illegally. Getting a truck out of the camp to pick up the cow was also illegal. Nevertheless, we found a Jewish driver who was willing. We picked up the cow and started back to camp, where we had to pass through a gate next to the barracks where the U.S. Army guards slept. We stopped the truck and got some people to push the truck through the gate and by the barracks.

Then came another trick—to keep the cow quiet while we unloaded it. We tied up its mouth and slid it down on boards. Then we needed a *shochet*, or butcher, to kill the cow in a kosher manner. By that point we had asked favors of so many people that nothing was going to be left for us. Six different people had claims on this one poor cow's liver. We had much more trouble with this transaction than it was worth.

We decided that any future cow killing would have to be done at the farmer's place, and we would sell the meat as non-kosher. When we ar-rived at the farmer's, he said it was up to us to kill the cow. It was only then that I learned Bernie did not know the first thing about killing, skin-ning, or butchering a cow. I had stupidly believed a butcher's son would have inherited his father's skill.

"Look," we told the farmer. "We're Jewish. Our religious views pre-vent us from killing cows."

"Well," he said, "if I kill it for you, you go ahead and butcher it. But save the cow hide for me."

He slit the throat of the cow, and we hung it up by the legs, head down. We started by skinning it, but we made a mess because we had no idea what we were doing. The worst part was yet to come. This would be opening up the cow and taking out its insides. I kept thinking Bernie might know something, but we just got deeper and deeper into making a mess. We finally sliced up the cow, but we vowed never to butcher one again.

When we got back to camp with the meat, it sold immediately. Everyone wanted more liver for their kids, but we only had so much. The next week we went back to the same farmer. We got more cows, but now we needed professional butchers. We found two who were much older than we were, and we made them partners in this venture.

Now the lines to buy our meat were even longer than we had ever hoped for. We were making bundles of money and we employed numerous workers. People began to place their orders with us, and we became the providers of fresh meat for the whole camp. But it was impossible to please everybody. Furthermore, the business was risky. Only the Austrian government was supposed to sell meat. Because I was willing to take risks, I was able to supply fresh meat in the camp. People who had a hot plate could cook a real dinner. When parents would bless me because I sold them liver for their children, that was worth more to me than the money and made the risks worthwhile.

OUR FIRST FARMER told us of others who wanted to sell their cows. On a snowy winter afternoon, one of my partners and I were skiing through a field on the way to a prospective purchase at a farm. An Austrian police patrol spotted us. They kept moving, and so did we. About a month later, as I was boarding a bus to Linz, I was taken off the bus by the Austrian police and transferred directly to their police station.

"Why am I here?" I asked.

"You were buying cattle illegally," one of them said.

"Who, me? I'm no butcher. I don't know the first thing about cows."

"We'll see."

They brought in the farmer who sold us our first cow, and my knees began to shake. I must have turned as white as the walls around us. But when the farmer looked at me, I saw that he felt sorry for me.

The Austrian policeman looked at the farmer.

"Is this the fellow?"

The farmer shook his head no.

I wanted to kiss him right then and there.

I was free to go, but he got six months of hard labor for selling cows illegally. When he was serving his term, I would see him on the highways and slip him things like cigarettes. If not for his pity for me, I would have been in jail.

The black market continued to be a thrill for us. If there was an item to be traded or sold profitably, we had it. We bragged that we could acquire most anything. People regarded us as a mobile market.

Many years later, a woman named Marsha whom I met in New York told me that most of the Jewish girls in the D.P. camp were scared of us because of our reputation as shady businessmen. She said there was no way any one of them would have gone on a date with us if we had asked. For my part, that was no problem, because I was not about to ask out someone so innocent. I was interested in other kinds of women. But it was a little shocking to hear over twenty years later what my reputation was like, even though I clearly deserved it.

ONE AFTERNOON I got picked up and taken to the house of the head of the local Organization of the Secret Service (OSS), which was the American secret police operating in civilian clothes in Austria. Today, they would be known as agents for the Central Intelligence Agency. The OSS was charge with overseeing American interests in their zone of Austria.

The chief OSS official in Enns had an Austrian girlfriend. He held up a piece of GI script.

"Do you know what this is?"

"No," I said. "I don't know a thing."

"Are you sure?"

"I just have time to mind my own business."

"Look, if you don't level with me, I'll put you in jail. What is the current price of script?" he asked.

"I don't know."

"I have 500 in script," he said. "I'd like you to buy it from me in Austrian shillings."

"I can't do anything like that. I'm not in business."

"Quit pulling my leg."

He had me in a tight spot. If I went along with him, I was committing a crime. If I didn't comply, he could have put me in jail anyway. By now I had learned the need to stay out of prison.

"I might know somebody in the business," I told him. "Maybe he could help us out if you let me handle the transaction. Give the money to your girlfriend and have her meet me in one hour. She can go with me to get the shillings."

"Fine," he said. "But if you double-cross me, I'll make it tough on you."

"Would I double-cross you? Where would I go?"

As it happened, he sincerely did want to do business with me. From then on he was a regular customer, but we were always very careful as to how we would meet.

The money kept coming in, and I had to work hard to spend it as fast as possible. Now the professional gamblers allowed me to play poker with them. We used to have a little "tea house" outside the camp, and we would all meet there to play cards. Once in a while my father would come to watch, and I would always lose more at those times. It was quite an honor to me to be perceived as an equal by these professional men. It used to hurt my father to watch me lose, and this would only make me a worse player. Years later I watched my son Robert lose a pot playing poker. I was ready to jump on him. Then I remembered my losses in the tea house, and I stopped myself from embarrassing my son in front of his friends.

# The Call
# to Palestine

I N  T H E  B E G I N N I N G  O F  1948,  R U M O R S  S T A R T E D
flying that Palestine was about to become an independent country
and that Britain was going to pull out its troops. The Jews were going to have a homeland. The Haganah or Zionist recruiters were looking for young men to volunteer and fight for this Jewish homeland. There
was a time when I would have been the first to volunteer. When I was in
Poland, I used to dream of going to Palestine. Even the first year I was in
Austria, there would have been a chance. But by now there was no way
I would give up the life I had. The business was big and everyone I dealt
with, even my partners, were older than I. I had plenty of money and lots
of women. I was riding high. Very high. Palestine fit nowhere into my
plans. But organizations like the Stern Group were making it tough on
those who refused. Rumors flew that they shot guys who would not go.

One night after a business transaction, Aaron, Bernie, and I came
back at one o'clock in the morning to the camp. A bunch of Romanian
and Hungarian guys who intended to fight in Palestine were waiting for
us with knives.

"Please put away your knives," I said. "You can come to our committee room and discuss what you want."

"We want you to go to Israel with us tomorrow morning," they said.

"We won't be forced to go," Aaron replied.

Some of the senior members of our camp overheard the conversation and rushed up to us. We had all been in the camp for as long as two years, whereas these Romanians and Hungarians had only been there a few months. But the older camp members were apparently persuaded by the sight of knives.

"You have no choice in the matter," one of the senior camp leaders said to us.

"But what about you?" Aaron demanded of them.

"We don't have to go. We are too old."

We had trusted these older men, but they did not trust us. They were for tying us up and transporting us that very night, all the way to Salzburg, a point of rail to Italy, and from there by boat to the Middle East. Of course, my group was surprised by this reaction. We had helped these older men out with petty cash, food, and supplies and done them many favors over a two-year period. Nevertheless, they were enough afraid of these newcomers that they now insisted we go to Palestine. They even woke up one of the camp drivers and asked him to come to the committee room. They wanted him to drive us all the way to Salzburg, right then and there. This driver had worked for us transporting cows, and we had paid him a lot of money. He looked at us and then shrugged at the elders.

"There's not enough gas in the truck," he said. "At this hour, I can't get any either."

The elders turned toward us. "Give us your word that you won't escape," one of them said. "Promise us that you'll go to Palestine."

"We won't go anywhere tonight," Aaron said. "In the morning we'll go to Palestine."

In the morning our psychology suddenly shifted and we changed our tactics. Instead of seeing the Romanians and Hungarians as our enemy, we joined forces with them to round up others who were in hiding and who should have been recruited to go to Palestine. We didn't want to leave any able bodies behind since we had been forcibly recruited. It was like war all over again, with everything changing in an instant.

We found three guys and came back to camp. We packed up for the journey and said good-bye to our parents and friends.

When our families cried, we started to get cold feet. We quickly devised a plan to jump off the train at Salzburg. In case we could escape the camp before boarding a truck for Salzburg, we also had a taxi waiting for us in Enns.

It came time for us to leave the next day. We loaded our suitcases onto an American army truck. Nearly 150 of us stood ready to get onto the trucks when OSS officers suddenly appeared and parked their car right in the middle of the gate. They got out and said there was no way we were going to be transported in American army trucks to wherever we might be going.

"You will have to hire civilian trucks," they told the people in charge. Soon we were unloading everything. Later, we learned that the mother of one of the recruits had telephoned the OSS and told them that American trucks were being used to transport us against our will.

My mother was standing near my truck. When the unloading began, she took my suitcase from me and started for our room in the camp. Then another mother did the same thing, and enough confusion was created so that no one really knew who was coming or going.

My friend Boniek and I, along with another guy who was a teacher, slipped into the camp hospital and then out through the windows. The back fence was not closely guarded by the Romanians and Hungarians, so we slipped through it and hid in some bushes. We asked an Austrian to go and get a taxi for us. We waited many hours, and after it was dark a taxi finally came and took us toward the resort town of Bad Ischl. We arrived at 3:30 a.m. and found out we could not get a room.

We boarded a train and tried to sleep. All of a sudden, the train was moving and we were headed toward the Russian border. Nothing could be worse than being caught there, because it would mean going back to Russia. Fortunately, we woke up and jumped off the train. Then we had to walk a few miles back to Bad Ischl. This time we were able to find a hotel room and we checked in and planned not even to leave our room for two weeks. We were sure we were the only three healthy guys left who did not go to Palestine. We were also afraid that if the Stern Group spotted us, they would shoot us as deserters, because by this time we knew they were very tough characters.

After only two days of hiding, we began to think of getting out of that room. Eating and playing cards, eating and playing cards—this was not something that was easy for our group. Finally, one day we sneaked into the park. We were shocked to discover nearly two hundred Jewish men walking in the park with their women. There they were, right out in the open, these healthy guys. Somehow they too had managed to escape the recruiters. These people all looked so comfortable, and here we were in our sweaty clothes that we had been wearing for days. We couldn't go to the store to buy new clothes, because there was nothing to buy.

We got word back to our camp that we needed clothing. Then we began to plan very carefully how to manage a trip to pick it up. We took a taxi at night and drove to Enns and to the designated place outside the camp in Enns. Right on schedule, my father threw a couple of suitcases over the fence. We went back to Bad Ischl without getting caught. We had lots of money, and now, with our clean clothing, we could start living in style.

When we came back to camp, we learned that there had been a trial to condemn our actions. The elders' committee decided among themselves to hold court and pass judgment on what they saw as desertion. Most of the other young people in our camp had "volunteered" to go to Palestine. Aaron was no young guy, of course, and he didn't even escape with us, but he was also "convicted."

No one was to speak to us or to our parents. We were ignored completely. If we ever got to Palestine, we would be court-martialed and sentenced as deserters. Father had made a statement at the camp trial to the effect that my two partners and I had every reason to run. We had too much to lose to go and get killed in another war. We were young and independent, Father said, and this should be no crime. I am glad that my father stood up for us. He understood how much we had all been through and how good our lives were now after so much misery. But this made the elders really angry and they ostracized us anyway.

Fortunately for us, the Enns camp was about to be closed officially, and all refugee residents were to move to another camp near Linz called Camp Ebelsberg. This place was larger and had better facilities. It was the Americans' idea to close three smaller camps like the one we were in and to move everyone to the larger camp. With Israel's independence in 1948, the need for waiting to go to Palestine had disappeared. Israel was open for all Jews to immigrate, despite problems of housing and transportation. So the D.P. camps had to be consolidated because the Jews were leaving for the Promised Land, Israel. This could not have come too soon. After all, being a displaced person was not something to be proud of.

Busy with settling into a new camp, everybody forgot about what had happened in Enns, and I became involved in many new business opportunities. It was simple. We were close to Linz, which was a much larger city than Enns; it was the biggest city in the American zone of Austria, so there were many more potential customers. I became part of a burgeoning wholesale cigarette business and had to take on two more partners. Now we were five. We opened up a regular wholesale house in a basement in the camp. We used to have regular salesmen on commission to bring Austrian customers to our warehouse. We bought coffee and sugar by the carload.

Our business was getting bigger and bigger, and we had to look to Vienna for merchandise. One of my partners suggested I go there to do some business. But it would be necessary to cross into the Russian-occupied Austrian zone, and for that, a false document was needed. A student card was the easiest to get, and of course, I looked the most like a student. Once we got the student document, my partners had devised a plan: a girl and I would travel as brother and sister to Vienna. She would carry the money in her panties. My partners made me promise I wouldn't fool around with my companion until after we had completed our business.

The daughter of one of our truck drivers was to be my "sister." This sounded fine to me, and so I agreed to all the terms and prepared to go. When I got to the cab, I opened the door and looked inside. In the light, all I could see was a fantastic pair of legs. I was breathless; the rest of her was just as beautiful. I hadn't seen anyone so lovely for weeks, and I stuck my head out of the cab and told my partners that I took back my promise. But they told me it was too late. I had given my word.

Normally we arranged to buy as many American cigarettes as possible, then we transferred them in trucks with false bottoms. The trucks would haul vegetables or some other commodity on top of the contraband. We would transfer money in the tire tubes, and no one would have to cross the border with money.

In this particular situation, our partner Bernie was in Vienna. A connection had fallen through, and we needed to get cash to him in order to buy cigarettes. Most of the time when there was a sticky situation or some traveling to do, I was the guy who would stick out his fearless neck. Once again, I pulled the trip off and transferred the money. Then this beautiful girl and I had a week in Vienna all to ourselves.

Meanwhile, my parents found out where I had gone. My mother was very upset. She was terrified when she imagined my getting caught by the Russians. Naturally, this did not stop me. Our business was dangerous and risky. One day, we would make a quick thousand dollars and the next day lose two thousand. I went to Vienna a few more times, until on one trip the Russians stopped the train and took off twenty-four Jewish guys. The only thing I could do was pretend I was asleep. Maybe the evening light protected me, because they didn't spot me, but I think it was another miracle. This was the last time I would make the trip to Vienna.

The bigger our business got, the bigger the risks and hazards became. One night we were expecting a truck with a shipment at three in the morning. We had arranged which gate to use to get the truck inside Camp Ebelsberg. Someone probably saw the truck and called the OSS. When we saw the OSS meet the truck, we kept right on driving. At the time, I had a jeep that looked like a station wagon. The officials stopped the truck and looked at it, but they couldn't figure out why a load of vegetables—I think it was cabbages—would be coming into camp at such an hour. Soon they had the truck at headquarters and were unloading it, and they found the cigarettes. There went our investment of $500. What could we do? Nothing.

Another time, Isaac came running to me and said the OSS was raiding our warehouse. By the time we got there all we could do was stand and watch. They confiscated thousands of dollars in coffee, sugar, and more cigarettes. This was our biggest warehouse, full of things impossible to get on the open market.

# Adultery

A FTER OUR BRUSH WITH THE STERN GROUP WE knew that the question of Palestine would not simply go away. Father knew I did not want to go, and he did not want the rest of the family to go. He went and registered us for immigration to the United States. He registered me separately for reasons of his own, and we all really didn't think anything would come of it. There were strict quotas for Polish people, and we knew everybody wanted to go to America. Father actually thought we would go to Australia. Australia was a large country with not too many people, and that sounded good to me. I was actually upset that he registered me for U.S. immigration without asking me first. So I told him that he and the family could go to America, but that I wanted to stay in Austria.

I was keen on spending my money on sporting events. There was no sport going on that I didn't attend, even if it was two hundred kilometers away. Our camp had its own football and boxing team, named Hakoa, and of course we would battle the Austrians, which was one of the reasons I liked going. They had three times as many policemen on duty when we played against them. Father thought my watching sports was a waste of time. I would often leave my warehouse and take the afternoon off, and he would think me so lax. We did have one partner who was stealing us blind, and father knew this. I guess he was right. Still I was much more interested in watching sports than in minding my business twelve hours a day.

I went to Salzburg once to see a famous British actress who starred in the first film production of *Hamlet*. This was during a film festival held in Salzburg. I went with a friend; we paid $150 for dinner and champagne at the Winkler Café. In those days, that was a lot of money just to go to a reception, but it was worth it. I got a chance to dance with the actress, and I appeared in my pinstripe suit dancing with her in a newsreel that was shown before feature films in Austria.

When a new ballerina or singer came to the opera, I had to have a date no matter what. If she was pretty, I would do anything just to be seen walking with her. Even though I did not always go to bed with these women, I wanted to be seen on the street with them. After the show at night, I would take them window-shopping and tell them they could come back tomorrow and buy whatever they wanted if they were nice to me tonight.

I was always looking for a challenge. Married women, of course, were the ultimate challenge. Besides, I knew I had less chance of getting venereal disease from them. Should a married woman get pregnant, she could always blame it on her husband. But then something happened to force me to change my mind.

We had a very good customer named Heinz, and one day he announced that he was going to get married. He wanted to show us a picture of his bride, but my partner warned him about showing a beautiful woman to me. Heinz laughed and said in jest that Henrich is okay. Whatever is mine, he can have. Heinz did not realize that I took him seriously.

Heinz and his bride got married and moved to the Russian zone. He was one of our top operators in the Russian zone, and he traveled a lot for us. One time, he informed us he was sending his wife with a communication for us, and we were to meet her in Linz. Usually, we would conduct business in the privacy of a hotel because everything we did was illegal. I met her at a hotel. The photograph of her that Heinz had shown me did not do her justice.

I had trouble finding a hotel room, so as a backup I rented a cabin on a ship that was in the harbor. Because of room shortages in Linz, boat owners on the Danube rented out their boat cabins like hotel rooms. I ordered us a bottle of wine, because she seemed nervous about the business and I wanted her to relax. We were talking about business when she mentioned that she had been married for three months. She said Heinz was constantly on the go, and they had no kind of sex life. That was like waving a red flag in a bull's face. Before I knew it, we were in bed making love, and this began our way of mixing business with pleasure. Heinz again had her deliver messages and money to us, and I would always be the one to meet her. We met again and again at hotels or in ship cabins.

I will never forget waking up in the room I shared with Isaac in Ebelsberg and seeing Heinz standing over me with a big knife. I can tell you one thing, he was no Abraham and I was no Isaac. His jaw was clenched.

"You got my wife pregnant," he said.

"Heinz, you're crazy," I said.

"She is pregnant with your baby," he said. "She told me all about it and admitted that it was you who got her this way."

"No woman is worth killing a man for," I told him. "Besides, if you kill me, you'll never get out of the camp. You'll have to kill Isaac, too, and he's innocent."

"Okay," he said. "Not today. But if I ever see you again outside the camp, watch out."

My partners also wanted to kill me after they heard what I had done with this good customer's wife. I felt bad about what it did to our business. I made a solemn oath never to have affairs with customer's wives or customers of any kind. This is an oath I have kept throughout my life. This incident also cured me of having affairs with married women.

THE BLACK MARKET business was very appealing. I had my own schedule, which allowed me to pursue good times whenever I wanted. Moreover, there was always some excitement. We were approached at any place at almost any time. One day, in the Linz railroad station, a man came over to me and asked me if I was interested in buying platinum.

I had never heard of platinum before, but a big shot like me was not going to admit this, so I told him that I was interested. He said he had some to sell, so we began walking toward our hotel. I was hoping that during this walk I would run into someone I knew who could tell me what platinum was.

Luckily, we ran into one of my partners, and I told the other guy I would stay with him while my partner went to check out the value of platinum. My partner couldn't find anyone to help him until someone suggested that he ask a dentist.

The dentist looked at a sample and said he had no way of testing the metal, but his guess was that because of the weight it was a pure product. Then he said that platinum was worth more than 24-karat gold, but that the only market for it was in France. This dentist, however, was willing to trade us 24-karat gold for an equal amount of platinum. This was because 24-karat gold was the gold used by dentists in Europe at the time, and he had a good supply of it.

My partner came back and reported all this to me. We knew that selling gold would be no problem because we had some experience with it. We offered to pay the platinum dealer twenty percent of the price we knew we could get for the gold. He was happy with that, and on this first deal, we made a profit of $800! That was a lot of money in 1948. Afterwards, we put this guy up in a hotel and began to drink with him and asked him if he could do more business with us. After a sumptuous feast, which included several bottles of wine, he began to tell us his secrets. He had been a chemical engineer in a chemical factory during the war. When the Germans began losing, they started to dismantle their factories, and all the employees helped with the work as long as possible in order to get paid. One evening, as he was leaving his factory, he kicked at some screening material in his path and noticed it was very heavy. He quickly figured out that it must have been platinum screening, used somewhere in the operation because it could withstand very high temperatures. He immediately got out some wire cutters and cut up some of the screen and put in into his rucksack and left work for the day. In all the confusion, no one paid any attention to him.

When the war ended, he was still an engineer, but he could not get a job in his profession. He had only odd jobs, which did not let him earn enough to support his family. So he decided one day to try to sell the screen platinum that he had rolled into balls and buried in the ground. He had heard that Jews in Linz were making a market in jewelry. He felt lucky that he had found me.

Little by little, he brought the platinum to us. He would tell us when to expect him, and my partners and I kept a sharp eye out for his train because we did not want him to sell to anyone else. We had too good a thing going not to protect it carefully. This man was our angel, and we treated him like one. During this time, my partner, Issie, got permission to leave for Canada, and one of the first things he did was write us a letter to say that we could be selling platinum for about three times the price of 24-karat gold. About then, our angel reappeared, and we made our largest purchase, only this time we did not sell all of it. As a matter of fact, I personally kept a good amount for myself. When I came to the United States, I carried it with me. Before I left, I ordered a custom-made pair of high-heeled shoes — these were fashionable at the time — and I had the shoemaker fit the platinum, which is very malleable, into a hollow space in the heels. Eventually, I sold it for $2,600.

FATHER WAS NOW A regular customer of ours, only it was difficult for me to deal with him. I had my partners do that. He only bought things he felt comfortable selling, which, of course, was the opposite of us, because we bought and sold anything.

Father ran a one-man operation. He supported his family and had saved more money than I had. He wouldn't think of blowing a lot of money on one night, the way I did. Fifty to a hundred dollars was a lot of money on the streets of Linz in 1948, and that is what I would spend. There were always bad feelings on this subject between the two of us. I enjoyed making and spending money, and I liked the adventure of doing business.

WITH THE CONTINUED growth of the camps, relations became even more strained among the camp residents, the police, and the townspeople. In 1949 tensions increased when Austrian police came into the camp to arrest someone. They brought in two busloads of police, about 100 men, which was far more than they needed, and they carried out the raid on a Saturday. A very religious group from Hungary was in the middle of Sabbath prayers in their shul. The entire camp was upset and resisted the Austrian police. All our hostility against Austrian anti-Semitism surfaced, and we routed the Austrians. From then on, the Austrian police never came back into our camp. They would send the OSS if necessary; they themselves preferred to deal with us outside the camp.

The Austrian civilian population was wary of us because they recognized how fearless we were. They knew we were not worth tangling with because we were fighting every minute of every day to survive. We had been toughened by all that we had been through, and they were no match for us. I could not do today what I did then for the simple reason that I would not have the guts. Maybe I used them all up, because today I don't feel I have any left.

Back then, the residents in the camps slowly regained their courage. Little things happened that made all the Jews feel that we as a people were somebody again. Israel was taking shape as a nation, and soon the people in the camps were demanding basic things, like enough firewood for heating. In our camp, the refugees actually began to tear down barracks for heating wood until the U.S. Army had to step in peacefully to restore order. From then on the camps had plenty of firewood, and this proved to the people in the camps that it was necessary to stand up for what we needed to survive. Today, of course, this spirit has taken root in Israel.

The U.S. CARE package became a big commodity for us. On top of rations there were these packages that we were supposed to receive once a week. It was easy to claim more packages than one should have, and, of course, I became involved in buying and selling CARE packages. My partners and I would get identification cards from refugees passing through to other camps and so would get the extra CARE packages delivered. Then it was only a matter of selling them on the black market for the going price of five dollars. Each one of us saw himself as pitted against the world, and together we formed a partnership. Being able to obtain something was the key, and how you got your hands on it was secondary. Honesty or dishonesty was beside the point. I would not think in such a way today, but in those days everything was okay. I saw myself as a displaced person without a country. The laws of Austria did not apply to me. The laws I adopted were the laws of supply and demand — and the laws of survival. The only merchandise I refused to deal in was dope. Dealing in dope was like murdering a human mind. No way I would sell it, ever.

The law of supply and demand was dictated by the desires of the moment. We stole goods, we stole women, and we understood the lawlessness of the war. The morality of all this doesn't measure well from a distance. Maybe one has to be there, both in the time and the place, to understand. All that I did sounds terrible today, but at the time I just wanted to be a big shot, to be recognized as a person. My father was concerned that all of my activities would eventually catch up to me, but from my vantage point, he was old and worried. I was lucky and young, and if you wanted something you had to depend on yourself to get it. This was something he had taught me. Even if he didn't approve of all my actions, at least he knew I could take care of myself.

IN MAY 1949 I WAS swimming in money and became serious about an Austrian girl. Her father had three trucks. That was considered a fleet in those days. Her name was Anna and she was different from most of the girls I took out. She was part Jewish, a small part, from her great-grandmother. She was a little shy and not very sexy, but her face was naturally very beautiful. Most of all, she was very smart. All in all, I could not say why I felt so strongly about her. After we had gone out for a while and made love, we became very close. Her father approved of me as a possible son-in-law. This was quite rare and special, given our very different religious backgrounds.

In July my father informed me that I was supposed to see the American consul in Linz. I was told that if I passed a medical examination, I would be going to America! This was a huge shock. I was not ready to go to America. I was used to calling my own shots by now. I told one of my partners that I didn't want to go because of Anna, and he went and told my father about her.

He was furious. You must remember that Hitler himself was an Austrian. For my father and other Jews there was really no difference between Germans and Austrians.

"If you marry this girl," he told me, "you'll be dead to me as a son." Of course this had just the opposite effect from what he intended. I was my own man at age twenty-one, and nobody, especially not my father Jacob Friedman, was going to tell me what I could or could not do.

MOTHER AND FATHER soon got permission to go to America. They were preparing to go, but I had convinced myself that I wanted to marry Anna. Mother broke out in tears every time she saw me. I wanted to please her, but there were many things holding me back. I enjoyed my partners and my business. In America I could expect to be a nobody, a manual laborer scraping by. I had grown accustomed to comfort, and I knew that America would be different. Then there was Anna and her father, both welcoming me to be part of their family. And of course there was my own sense of pride, not wanting to be told what to do by my father.

After many more tears, my mother got me to agree to go to America for one year. If I did not like it, then I could return to Austria. I felt very uncertain about this decision. One month before I was to leave I started to party every night. I was still considering marriage to Anna — until one night I met Inga in a cabaret. She was a cabaret dancer. Soon I stopped seeing Anna entirely. Inga was more my type. She was sexy and bitchy-looking, with a great imagination for sex. Because there was no question of marrying her, it took some worry off my shoulders.

Today I can close my eyes and still remember my last night in Linz. It was spent in the Metropolitan Cabaret Club. Nothing I could have dreamed up could match this night. The champagne flowed for me and my friends, and at two o'clock in the morning the owners kicked out everyone but our party. An hour later, Inga excused herself. Then suddenly all the lights went out. No one quite knew what was happening until right above me, there on our table, stood Inga, completely naked. A spotlight shone on her and she began to dance to a sexy melody. I had never heard this kind of music or seen this kind of dancing any place in Europe. Dancing on the table, in front of everyone, without really touching me, Inga made love to me. I knew Inga did this all just for me so that I would remember her especially. And believe me, to this moment I can still remember that unbelievable night in Linz.

# AMERICA

# Journey
# to America

W E LEFT LINZ BY TRAIN IN OCTOBER 1949.
When we arrived at the nearby city of Salzburg, we were put
up in a hotel. Mother, Father, and Mendel were in one room,
Isaac and I in another. We stayed in Salzburg for about three days. At
that time the United Nations Emergency Relief Assistance (UNERA) was
responsible for us. I had many friends in Salzburg, and spent two nights
at one of my favorite clubs called the Casanova.

During my first night there I met a very attractive woman. Since this
was going to be my last time with an Austrian woman, I tried to get a
room of my own. None were available, but since there were two beds in
the room I was sharing with my brother Isaac, I invited her to the hotel.
"I have a brother who is sound asleep in my room," I told her. "He won't
be a problem." The next morning, I put my brother outside the door to
watch for Father. Somehow, I managed to get her out of the room without his seeing her.

WE RODE IN A TRAIN full of refugees from Salzburg to Bremerhaven. Refugees from all over Europe were going to Bremerhaven, and

then to America. When we arrived in Bremerhaven we were put into a D.P. camp. These were again army barracks. We stayed for about one week there. Now I wanted to make love to a German girl.

I met a sixteen-year-old who was gorgeous. I persuaded her to go with me to a hotel so that I could make love to her as she had never been made love to before. "You will be very special to me," I told her.

We made love for hours. I ordered food through room service. We ate and drank the champagne and made more love. I did have to leave her for a short time to go back to the camp to report, so that nobody would be worried about me. My parents were, in fact, very worried. They figured I would stay out overnight, but they did not think that I would be gone most of the day also. I explained to them that I had gotten tied up with friends and that I would be gone for another night. When I went back to the hotel, however, the girl was gone. Nevertheless, it had been a great night for me to remember during my last moments in Europe.

Our stay lasted a few more days before we were put on board a huge ship, the *General Sturgess*, which was carrying many refugees. We were crowded into uncomfortable compartments for the two-week journey from Bremerhaven to Boston. This was in November, and the Atlantic Ocean was wild. My mother was very, very seasick. She kept crying and said if Columbus was such a great person, why did he have to discover a country that you could reach only by water? Why couldn't he find an America that you could reach by land? I still laugh about that statement because it was so typical of my mother.

I did not get sick, and I worked in the kitchen where there was plenty of food. When other passengers got sick, they refused to eat and therefore got weaker. I ate like a pig and never got sick.

I met black people for the first time on this boat ride. Many of the cooks were African Americans. They were very friendly to me. Originally we were scheduled to arrive in New York, but because there was a strike in New York, we had to land in Boston. That delayed our arrival by about two days.

It is hard now to describe the feeling of approaching the promised land, America. It was like reaching heaven on earth. Everybody was up very early that morning, anxious to see this land of the free, where all are considered equal.

IT WAS LATE on a dark November afternoon when we were processed through immigration in Boston. I was anxious because I was carrying platinum in the heel of my shoes. This was the platinum I had saved and had not exchanged for 24-karat gold. I was afraid of being frisked. My brother Isaac, who had taken English lessons, was the family interpreter, but he found out that learning English in Europe and speaking English in America were two different things.

A friend that I met on the boat had an acquaintance living in Boston who came to meet us at the immigration station.

"You won't believe it," he said to us.

"What?" my friend asked.

"We have television here."

"Television?" I asked. "What is television?"

"You have got to see it," he said.

We ran a couple of blocks to a store window and saw a screen, a picture, and a voice. He was right. I could not believe it. How was this possible? There was no projector, and yet a picture was coming through a wire. It seemed so astounding at the time.

The Hebrew Immigrant Aid Society (HIAS) was an American Jewish organization that took responsibility for us in Boston. After my family finished all their paperwork at the immigration office, we were taken to the train station and put on a train to Chicago. The HIAS gave us some spending money for meals; when we went to the dining room, however, we could not read the menu. We pointed to what we wanted after seeing what others were eating.

The most amazing thing to me was looking out the train window for cowboys and Indians and seeing none, not even a horse. All through the journey I kept hoping to see cowboys, but instead I saw parking lots full of cars and more cars. Even though I had a car in Europe, the majority of the people there did not. Most of the transportation was by bicycle, motorcycle, or train. Seeing all these cars was unbelievable to me. And they were just parked.

We arrived in Chicago on an extremely chilly December night. A couple of women from HIAS greeted us and took us in a taxicab to the next station stop, where we awaited a train to Seattle. We reached Seattle on a wintry day and were picked up by another woman, this time from the

Jewish Family and Child Service (JFCS), which sponsored us in Seattle. In order for us to come to America, a party or organization had to assume responsibility for us.

We were taken from the train station with our few belongings and put up at a hotel, the Haddenhall. We could see cracks in the walls of the hotel and wondered how old a building it was. Then we learned that Seattle had had a very severe earthquake just a few months before. "My God!" Mother said. "We came all this way to America to a city that has earthquakes."

That first Sunday we had visitors, a couple named Schlosinger who had been born in Germany. They were kind enough to take my brother and me for a ride and show us Seattle. I was very impressed. When I asked them for employment, Mr. Schlosinger offered to get me a job washing cars at the gas station where he was an attendant.

So on Tuesday of my first week in America, I started washing cars. I worked at this job for about three days and then I quit. I had hoped for a better opportunity than this. Besides, it was very cold. Father found a job as a painter for the Council of Jewish Women. The council was preparing to open a thrift shop in a building directly across from our hotel. In addition to painting, Father would also go around with a truck to collect old clothes and things that could be sold in the thrift shop.

It did not take us long before we were on our own and independent. Isaac enrolled in a high school and became a celebrity because of our family's survival during the war. There was an article about him in the school newspaper, and his story was even written up in the city's two major newspapers.

After washing cars, I found another job as a dishwasher in the coffee shop across the street from a department store. I worked at that job for one week, at the end of which time the owner gave me a check for two weeks' pay. He told me that I was not fit to do dishes. I was insulted. Here I had come to this great country, and I was told I couldn't even wash dishes. As a matter of fact, I missed Europe and did not like America.

Americans appeared crazy to me. They did not take two hours for lunch as people did in Europe. Here one started on the job early in the morning and had only half an hour for lunch. It struck me as utterly perplexing. In Europe we had heard America was the land of milk and honey — that people just put out their hands and the money fell in. People in Europe had no conception of how tough it could be living in America. We really only knew America from the movies, in which people seemed to have everything they needed.

We lived at the Haddenhall for about two weeks. I was very lonely, and I tried to figure out where someone could go dancing. I asked a person where to go "tancing," and he didn't understand me, so finally I demonstrated dancing a tango. "Oh," he said. "It's not very far. There is the Trianon Dance Hall." This place was just about six or seven blocks from our hotel.

That Saturday night I decided to go there. I spoke in broken English and I did not know how to ask a girl to dance. I tried to gesture clumsily with my hands. I will never forget what she said. "I can tell from your eyes what you want," she said. "You don't have to talk." Somehow I understood what she meant, and we had a lovely evening dancing together.

Soon after that I signed up to learn English at a language school. I found English very difficult, but I continued with the lessons.

My next job, which I got through the JFCS, was with a feather company. We used to bring in bales of chicken feathers and goose feathers, and we would sort them out and wash them in a huge washing machine. I would wear a mask to keep the feathers from flying into my face when they were dry. Even with the mask, I would have feathers in my eyes and my hair, my nose and my ears, you name it. This job didn't pay too badly. I worked there for about three months, till I moved on to a couple of jobs upholstering furniture. In desperation, I then took a job with Fisher Flour Company. Even though I was not making as much money as I had with my former jobs, the work was much cleaner and easier.

In the meantime, we had moved from the Haddenhall to an apartment my father found. We lived upstairs. Downstairs lived a family of refugees from Austria who had come to America on the same boat as we. Their daughter, a beautiful redhead, went out with many American boys. I would sneak into her room to make love to her and she would tell me about all the boys she was dating. I would advise her not to make love to them. She took my advice. Whenever I wanted to make love, she was available. She later moved to Las Vegas and became a showgirl, and she also had small parts in a couple of motion pictures.

I still hated America. Many of the American women I dated asked me why I didn't go back to Austria if I hated America so much. At the time I didn't realize what they meant, and I thought, what the hell do they know?

I had a group of friends, mostly refugees. Some were now in the U.S. Army. They were stationed at Fort Lewis, a few miles to the south, and they would often visit Seattle on weekends. Sometimes we would go out and look for girls; sometimes we played soccer.

# The Army
# and Korea

I N NOT QUITE TEN MONTHS, I HAD GONE THROUGH
six jobs. I was counting the days until I could go back to Europe,
but President Truman and the Korean War changed my plans. From
the outset, things had not gone as I'd expected in this country. When my
boat was sailing to America, I looked forward to being welcomed by the
Statue of Liberty, but because of a longshoremen's strike in New York
Harbor, we landed in Boston. I felt cheated that I had missed out on the
traditional greeting at Ellis Island. I did, however, receive my official
welcome in September of 1950 when President Truman sent me special
greetings—a draft notice to serve in the United States Army. I was suddenly faced with a difficult decision: I could go back to Europe, or I could
join the army.

I was miserable. I kept getting letters from my partners telling me
how much money they were making and what a great life they were having in Austria, which made me jealous. I felt that I didn't have much in
common with Americans my age because they seemed to me to be su-
perficial, unaware of how tough it can be in the real world.

The friends I did have were refugees like me. Some of them decided to go to college to avoid the service. Others were excused because they pretended not to know English. I wanted to get it over with, to see what would happen. On October 22, 1950, I was sworn into the U.S. Army, even though I was not a citizen of the United States. About seventy guys from the State of Washington were put on a train and sent to Fort Riley in Kansas for basic training.

I really learned about poker that night on the train. We didn't sleep. At times, I was way ahead in the game, but I was too stupid to quit. Or I didn't have the guts to quit. By morning, I was busted. I don't think I had three or four dollars on me.

I learned a couple of very important lessons from that night of playing poker. First rule: I would set aside a sum of money I could afford to lose and would never chase after lost money. My second rule was never to be broke again. I was in two camps within a two-month period, and I didn't get paid until the third month. And I didn't have the nerve to write home for money. So from that time on, I made sure I always had money.

When we arrived at Fort Riley, I experienced discipline for the first time. We were handled like animals, yelled at as if we were stupid. The weather was just miserable when we got there.

At the end of the first week we were told we were going to have a GI party Friday night. I was looking forward to that. It turned out that a GI party was scrubbing floors. What a shock! We had to clean the barracks for Saturday morning inspection. I had to eat the food the army served us, which was terrible, and the weather was *still* miserable.

After two weeks we were shipped to Camp Cook, California, to complete a division of the National Guard that had been activated into the regular army. Again, there was a long ride across the country. This time I didn't play poker! I didn't have any money.

The 40th Infantry Division of the National Guard, now a division of the U.S. Army, was headed to Europe. I was elated when I was chosen for a position (G-2) where I could make use of the many languages I spoke. By the time I got through with several interviews, I was told that after basic training I would be sent to a special school for languages near San Francisco. But first I had to learn to speak better English. All the people who came with me from Washington state were assigned to infantry. But I was assigned to artillery. I never did go to the language school.

Since our liberation in 1944, I had been my own man. The discipline that I had to contend with in the army was very hard for me, but somehow I think that the sergeants and the officers were a little easier on me than they would have been on an American kid. Before long, I was doing things that I liked. I was in the fire direction center, which I enjoyed because it had to do with mathematical calculations. I would compute at what elevation the big guns should fire to hit the enemy.

My first experience of anti-Semitism in the army occurred when one of the soldiers called me a "kike." I went berserk. It was the only time I was in a fight while in the army. No one got hurt, but from then on the guys respected me. After all the suffering I had witnessed because of my Jewishness, I simply could not accept anti-Semitism, especially not as a member of the U.S. Army.

My outfit was supposed to be going to Europe. At the last minute we were ordered to Japan instead. This was a shock and a terrible disappointment to me.

My English had improved considerably by this time. I was considered knowledgeable enough to speak to the company about crises or important situations that involved America around the world. Because communism was perceived as the enemy, and I was a survivor of both Nazism and communism, my commander asked me to speak to the troops of my experiences. I guess I was good. They made me tell my story to the whole division, and when we landed in Japan, I became one of the guys assigned to discuss current events. I had to write my speeches in advance, and then I would give them to a sergeant in my outfit who would type them up for me and correct my misspellings and poor grammar. I was proud, however, to be chosen to address my peers.

It took us about two weeks to reach Yokohama. The day we arrived, General Douglas MacArthur was fired by President Truman. We were all stunned. General Matthew Ridgway was going to take over as commander of the United Nations forces in Korea and the Allied occupation forces in Japan.

We disembarked from the ship and took a train to the camp, which was about four hours from Yokohama. We got there toward evening and straightened out our barracks and our equipment. The next morning we came out to the gate to see where we were and found that a small village surrounded our compound. The first words I learned were "GI you want pam pam?" This meant "Do you want to make love?" After about two months we moved to Camp McNeil at the bottom of Mount Fuji. We were there another two to three months.

ONE EVENING IN A night club in Tokyo, I saw a beautiful Japanese woman playing the piano. Her name was Joy. I asked some guys who were stationed in Tokyo if they knew her. They did, but they also told me she was very strict and did not associate with GIs at all. I took this as a challenge. When I offered to buy her a drink, she refused. So I waited until she got through and tried to talk to her. She told me that dating American GIs would ruin a Japanese girl's reputation. "I'm really not that kind of GI," I said. "I'm from Europe, which makes me different from the Americans." She was not impressed.

I decided to bribe one of the waiters to get her address for me. I took a taxi to her house the next day, and brought coffee, sugar, and candy, items difficult to find in Japan at that time. When I got to her house, she was so embarrassed she almost fainted. Still it would have been very impolite for a Japanese to turn down someone who brings gifts. Joy's father had served in Manchuria and had learned Russian, so we were able to communicate in that language. I told him my story, and he came to like me. At that time, I really thought I was in love with his daughter.

After a while Joy moved near the camp, and I got her a job playing piano at the base because she was an excellent pianist and a good entertainer. I used to bring gifts to her parents, and we talked a lot about the war. She had two younger sisters. Her parents seemed to accept me as a future son-in-law. They were not ashamed of me because I was very good to her. I also felt safe making love to just one woman.

Joy lived with me for the duration of my stay in Japan. She never raised her voice to me. My parents had many arguments, and as a child I accepted that that was what happens when a man and woman live together. But with Joy there were never arguments. I would come home, filthy from a day in the field, and a hot bath would be waiting for me. She would soap me up and rinse me down.

The Japanese at that time were very poor. It was always shocking to me how many people lived together in one small room. They would cook in the room, and then they would bed down in that same room. It was hard for me to understand how little space the Japanese had. Every little piece of land was cultivated. Their homes, no matter how small, were exceptionally clean. I meticulously observed their custom of removing one's shoes before entering the house. My ten months in Japan went by very fast.

In December 1951, the 40th Infantry Division received orders to replace the 24th Infantry Division in Korea. I was one of the guys selected to go as an advance party to take over the 24th's equipment. Most of us were depressed. We had heard what happened to the 24th. Most of them got wiped out. They lost their colors to the Chinese and North Koreans, and they were badly beaten up. Now we had to go into a hell hole and defend South Korea.

On Saturday nights, we would go out and get drunk. Meanwhile, Joy was very upset with me. I became increasingly difficult to get along with. I was mad at my parents for forcing me to come to America. I could have gone to Israel and at least died fighting for a Jewish state. In America I was not even a citizen, but I had been sent thousands of miles to be killed in a forsaken place like Korea. Joy decided to go back to Tokyo to live with her parents.

I T   T O O K   A  good month before the 40th Infantry Division could take control of the area and the 24th could go to Japan. Our positions were about five miles behind the front lines. Because we were in artillery, our range was about seven and a half miles. We had 105 howitzers. My responsibility was to check the equipment, compile an inventory, and sign off for what we were getting.

At night I slept in a bunker with five other people. The bunker was dug into the ground and sandbagged. The six bunks were made out of wooden ammunition boxes. There was an oil stove right in front to keep the place warm. We slept in sleeping bags and used our clothes for pillows.

It was miserably cold and there was a shortage of water. In order to bathe, we had to go outside and fill our helmets with snow, put them on the stove to melt the snow, and then wash ourselves with that water. In the morning it would be thirty-two below zero, but we didn't care. We just moved very fast.

When the rest of the outfit arrived, we had to dig into new positions for temporary placement. There would be a shortage of space until the

24th Division moved on to Japan. The ground was frozen and it was very hard to dig. We blasted holes with a hand grenade, or dug a small hole, put in a bit of blasting powder, and blasted away. We set up pup tents in these little spaces and slept four in a tent. We woke up each morning covered with ice and frost. It was difficult to get out of the sleeping bags because we slept with our clothes on and the frozen bags stuck to them. The only thing we took off at night was our boots. I would think to myself: "My God, after all I went through . . . "

I took responsibility for supplying our guys with "goodies." I would collect their money and make a beer run to Seoul, scrounging from the navy and the air force because they always had enough beer. I would buy as many cases as I had money for. Ours was the best-supplied outfit when it came to beer. Oftentimes, too, guys wanted to buy cameras, and there was a shortage of these at our post exchange. So I would find ways to get them.

I wrote my mother and told her some of the things I was doing. She wrote back, "Don't you dare do the things that you are thinking of doing." My mother wrote in Yiddish and the words rhymed humorously. I have never forgotten that letter. She was afraid that if I did black market business, I would get caught and never become a United States citizen. I would go to prison and be dishonorably discharged. My mother was able to read my mind.

After about four or five months into our time in Korea, many mothers and wives complained to the government about sending the 40th and the 45th Infantry Divisions to a battle zone. Members of the National Guard were not supposed to be sent out of the country. They were supposed to protect the shores of the United States in cases of emergency.

We received a visit from Governor Earl Warren of California. Right after his visit, most of the original National Guard boys from California were sent home. We draftees, who had been activated with the 40th Division into the regular army, were the only ones left.

In all the time I was in Korea I was shot at only three times. Once our own planes mistakenly strafed our positions. The second time was during an ambush from machine guns. And the third time, a bullet zipped past me from a sniper ridge.

After a horrible winter, we were faced with summer typhoons. In August 1952, some of us who were to be discharged in September began counting the days. We were short-timers. We dreamed of driving on smooth highways without chuckholes, of being with family, and of sleeping in real beds. I wanted to take a shower or a bath more often than once a month. I dreamed of having a real steak with baked potatoes and of sleeping, just sleeping, for days.

# The Jewelry
# Business

I N  O C T O B E R  1 9 5 2 ,  I  B O A R D E D  A  B O A T  B A C K  T O
the United States. Seventeen hundred guys were jammed into a ship
that was supposed to carry only eight hundred people. The voyage
lasted twelve days. Even before we arrived in the Port of Seattle, an
announcement came over the loudspeaker: "Now hear this. Now hear
this. All gentlemen from the State of Washington and the city of Seattle,
please assemble in the hull of this ship." I was one of fifteen men from
Washington. We were told to be ready when the time came to disem-
bark, because we were to be photographed by the press and interviewed
soon after we arrived in Seattle. I was the first one off the boat.

I was discharged from the army on October 21st at Fort Lawton, ten
days after my arrival in Seattle. My first order of business was to buy
clothes and a brand new baby-blue Chevrolet, for cash. My first Saturday night as a civilian, I went out to have a good time with a buddy from
Tacoma who had also served in the 40th Infantry Division. When I got
home Sunday morning, my father told me that Albert Klein had called
me about a job.

A few days earlier, I had been invited to the Jewish Club of Wash-

ington, which consisted of refugees from Europe. When I was introduced by the president of the club, I stood up and thanked everybody for
the warm welcome, but I told them that I needed a job. Mr. Klein, a
wholesale jeweler, was a member of the club.

That particular Sunday a job was the furthest thing from my mind.
I had a terrible hangover, and all I wanted to do was sleep. I called
Mr. Klein, however, and made an appointment to meet him that same
evening. I went to his apartment and met his wife. As I was leaving he
told me he had to interview one other person, but his wife smiled and
told me not to worry, I had the job. As things turned out, I would work
for Mr. Klein nearly eight years.

He taught me the value of hard work and how to be a good salesman. My territory, which I shared with Mr. Klein's brother, Ludwig, included parts of Washington, Oregon, Idaho, and northern California.
We sold wholesale fine jewelry: watches, wedding rings, diamond rings,
watch bands, gold-filled items—and some fashion jewelry, a stylish and
elegant version of what had once been termed "costume jewelry." In the
early 1950s, fashion jewelry was again becoming popular, and we had a
supplier in Germany. We would have one little case, but there would be
twenty different styles to sell. We were also selling Elgin compacts and
other gift items to jewelry stores.

I remember showing the line, and the owner or buyer would say
"Give me one of this and one of that." Mr. Klein would write down *three*.
The owner would see my embarrassment and would just smile.

Later, I asked Mr. Klein, "How could you write three pieces when
sometimes they only ask for one?"

"I know what he needs," he said. "I know what he can use. He
doesn't know."

On my next trip I asked this customer, "How come you didn't
object when you asked for one piece and Mr. Klein gave you three
pieces?"

"Well," he said to me, "if I told Mr. Klein three pieces, he would
have written six pieces. I know how he writes. He pushes the pencil. So
that's the reason I told you only one piece."

MR. KLEIN TAUGHT ME that you have to know your customers
and how much they are likely to need. Underselling is as bad as over-

selling. You don't want to leave a vacuum for your competitors to fill. I remember one visit to a jeweler in Brewster, Washington. After three months I was already working by myself, and as I walked in, the jeweler was just madder than hell. I asked him why.

"This Elgin watch salesman overloaded me with watches," he replied. "I don't know how I am going to sell all those watches. I have to pay all these bills. The next time this guy comes, I am going to throw him out."

The jeweler apologized for his very small order and told me that on my next visit he would give me a large order. I was one of the first salesmen on the road after Christmas, and I arrived in Brewster expecting a large order from this man.

'You know," the jeweler said, "the Elgin salesman was back again. I did real well with his watches last time, so I had to replace my stock. I can buy very little from you." The Elgin watch salesman was ahead of me.

I learned an important lesson. Because the jeweler had enough watches to sell, he was able to do more business. He was pushing harder because he had an obligation of paying promissory notes. He knew he had to sell all that merchandise. A good salesperson needed to know his customer, the territory, and the type of merchandise that would be best in a given store.

When I was with Mr. Klein on the road, he would work the entire day. After dinner he would add up all the orders. He would go to bed very late, after watching a little television to relax. He was always working. That was his hobby. He was a wonderful salesman because he knew his product and knew his customers.

Once, during my first year of selling, I was in the little town of Wilbur, on the way to Spokane. I was trying to sell diamond rings to the jeweler there. I pitched him very hard. He turned toward me and said, "You don't know what the hell you're talking about." I turned red. I was speechless. Finally I asked him if he'd like to have lunch.

"All right," he said. "I haven't even had coffee yet. Let's go."

Over lunch I learned that his wife had cancer, which explained his irritability. My mother was also dying of cancer at that time, so we had a subject we could share. After lunch I confessed to him that I had not been in the diamond business long. "I really don't know that much about diamonds," I told him.

"Oh, forget it," he said. "Let's see what you have anyway." I showed him my entire line, and he placed an order worth $725. That was a very big order in 1953, worth about $10,000 in 1998.

I was beginning to learn that a salesman has to think fast and not make statements that will put him in an awkward position. This takes years and years of experience. One of my customers in Boise, Idaho, was always about six months behind in making payments. He would give me promissory notes. I always accommodated him. Later, when he became a success, he always paid his bills on time. He also started buying from other people. One day it was very hot in Boise. I drove around until I could find a parking spot near the store, so I would not have to carry the cases too far.

"Hi, Hank," he greeted me. "How are you? You're late. Several other salesmen have already been here, and I just overbought. I don't know what to do with what I bought." I was angry because I always sent out a card at least two weeks before I arrived.

"You know something," I said. "I have sold you all these years when you were slow paying, and I stuck my neck out for you. Now when you are paying your bills, everyone wants to sell to you and you have forgotten your old friends. Even if you wanted to buy, I don't want to do business with you if you're going to be that way." I walked out of his store.

Two years later, in Medford, Oregon, I called on a good customer, and as I walked into the store, who do I see instead but the man who owned the store in Boise.

"Hello," I said. "How are you? What happened to Anderson?"

"I bought this place from him," he replied.

"Mr. Anderson was very successful with my jewelry in this spot," said I. "I hope you'll continue the tradition."

"You told me that you never wanted to do business with me again," he said. "Let's leave it that way."

I had learned another valuable lesson: You have control over your thoughts as long as you don't express them. Once they are on your tongue, they are beyond your control. Don't say anything to a customer that you may regret. Give him the respect he is entitled to. Use your head. Use your mouth only to sell the product.

I love selling. We all have to sell ourselves. I don't care if you're in show business, or a teacher. No matter what you do in a job, you have to sell yourself. You are the ambassador of your own destiny.

Generally, my trips would last two weeks. I would be away from home, and in those days there were no motels, so I would stay in hotels. One night I would have a room with a bath and one night a room without a bath, just a sink to wash in. I could not afford to have a room with a bath every night.

IN 1953 MY mother became very ill. She had surgery and was diagnosed with cancer. I remember going to the hospital after her surgery. When I walked into her room, she woke up and looked into my face.

"Be honest with me," she said. "Tell me the truth."

I had a very hard time telling her that she had cancer. But she kept insisting that I tell, because she could read it from my face. It didn't seem fair, after all that she had gone through in the Holocaust. She was still a young woman at fifty-one. Her child Mendel was only eight years old.

In August 1954 I took her to the hospital for the last time. She looked at her home and said, "I will never come back." Whenever I was in town, I would visit her at night and in the morning before I went to work. I used to say, "Mom, how are you doing? You're getting better."

"What's the matter?" she would ask. "Are you my enemy? Pray to God that I die."

To this day I have a difficult time going to a hospital. I had to live with a guilty conscience for many years, because the morning my mother died I did not go to the hospital. I had slept in and was shaving when they called to tell me that my mother was dead. I don't know why I felt so guilty. I felt maybe she wanted to tell me something. Maybe she wanted to talk to me, and I was not there. I lived with that for almost thirty years, until my mother-in-law was dying, and we were all crowding around her. The doctor took us outside her room to talk to us.

"Let the lady die in peace," he said. "When an animal wants to die, he walks away from the hurt so that he can die by himself. You are not giving her a chance to die. People want to die by themselves, not in a crowd."

I told him about my guilty conscience. "Your mother died because you were not there," he said. "She wanted to die in peace."

Mother, in the short time she lived in Seattle, had made a great many friends. At the funeral parlor, some of the women started screaming and crying and holding onto the coffin. She was buried in the Jewish Orthodox cemetery.

In a way, I felt good that Mother had passed on, because I could not stand to see her in pain. But in another way, I felt a tremendous loss. I had always been able to share things with her much more than I could with my father.

I WAS SPENDING a lot of time on the road. Usually I was gone on business at least four or five months each year. I was still quite a playboy at the time, and I prided myself on having a girl in every city. Very seldom would I admit to any woman that I was selling jewelry. If they asked me what I was doing in Boise, I would tell them that I was in the air force. I enjoyed the traveling, and I enjoyed meeting the different women.

When I came back to Seattle, I would have lined up a different woman every night. I loved to dance. As a matter of fact, I had a friend named Leon Mezistrano, and we used to go out a lot together. The only time we knew we were having a good time was when our shirts were all wet from dancing. I learned to dance by dating teachers from the Arthur Murray Dance Studios. After they were through working, I would take them to a night club and dance with them late into the night.

# Sandy

O NE AFTERNOON IN JUNE 1955, MY BUDDY
Leon and I were sitting in the kitchen of his mother's house.
We were discussing our dates of the previous evening. His
brother and his cousin were washing the cars.

"Why are they washing the cars here?" I asked.

"They're going to a wedding," he said.

"Whose wedding?"

"Raymond Benezra. He's marrying Joyce Feinberg."

I knew Ray.

Then Leon began to tell me about a girl he once dated, Sandy Bar-
nett, who almost broke his finger when he tried to make a pass at her. I
thought that sounded interesting.

"Why don't you call her up?" I said. I also suggested that he ask
Sandy if she knew Karen Klatzker, who was a pretty girl I'd met recently
in a coffee shop. I wanted to get to know Karen, so I could ask her out
sometime.

Leon called Sandy.

It turned out that Karen Klatzker was Sandy's cousin, and both of them were going to the wedding. Although we weren't invited, we decided to crash the reception. We would have a drink, meet the girls, and do a little dancing. When we arrived, Leon introduced me to Sandy and I introduced him to Sylvia Capelotto, whom I had taken out once or twice.

I danced with Sandy most of the evening, and she introduced me to her parents. I also met Karen for the second time, and I made a date to take her out when I was back in town.

Two weeks later, when I returned from my business trip, I had a phone message from Sandy. When I called, she told me that Karen had had to go out of town with her mother. I was disappointed, naturally, so I asked Sandy what she was doing. She agreed to go to a movie with me. Leon and Sylvia went with us.

Sandy was only eighteen at the time, five feet two, with a slender figure. We began dating regularly. Once on a shopping trip after work, I discovered that she had a positive influence on me. Usually, I'd buy half a dozen shirts and a suit or two, but with Sandy I wound up with only one sport shirt. I thought to myself, boy, here's the girl I need. I was making good money but was extremely loose with it.

Later that summer we went to another wedding, where I met Sandy's mother and father for the second time. Her mother was petite — she weighed maybe ninety-five pounds. Her father owned a restaurant and was a hard worker, getting up each morning at three o'clock. After the wedding party, we went to a lounge for some dessert and bumped into her parents again. Leon and I were leaving for a brief vacation the next day. I stayed up until about four o'clock in the morning with Sandy. I remember telling her that I thought that I was in love with her. Ninety percent.

Leon and I went to San Francisco, Los Angeles, and then Las Vegas. I found Las Vegas boring, whereas in the past I had always had a great time there. After a few days, we decided to go to Reno. We left that night, and I stopped in the desert at a gas station to call Sandy. We were in the middle of nowhere, but I needed to talk to her. We told each other how much we missed each other.

Leon was laughing. He thought I was crazy. We arrived in Reno late that night and couldn't find a place to stay in our price range. We dozed in the car and in the morning found a motel with a swimming pool. We spent a few days, but I was antsy. I just had to get back to Seattle. We drove all night, taking turns. We arrived in Seattle around ten o'clock in the morning. I took a nap, and then I called Sandy and told her I would like to talk to her.

"Sure," she said.

I didn't know what was happening to me. I had always had very good control over my emotions. When I arrived at Sandy's house, her parents were not home. We talked for hours. In the end I asked her if she would like to go steady.

"Does that mean we are engaged?" she asked.

"If that's what going steady means," I said, "then we are engaged."

I can claim today that not knowing the difference between the English-language phrases "going steady" and "being engaged" turned my life around, because all I wanted was to have a girl who belonged to me. But marriage was the furthest thing from my mind. Anytime a girl started suggesting marriage, I stopped seeing her. I was afraid of responsibility.

Within an hour Sandy's parents returned. They were very happy for us. Then we went to Sandy's big grandmother—called "big" because Sandy's other grandma was very little. We told her our intentions and she gave us her blessings. Then we went to see "little" grandma, Sandy's mother's mother. Here was a woman about five feet tall and weighing about sixty-five pounds, but she was as strong as steel and a tough cookie. She ruled the roost, so to speak. She was very *haimish*.

After we made our announcement, things started moving very fast. Leon and Sylvia also got engaged, and they were planning their wedding for March. I was introduced to Sandy's cousin, Caroline Backer, who soon became engaged to Herbert Schwartz, and the six of us became a package.

Sandy's parents were to select the site of the ceremony and reception. In Seattle in 1955 there were bad feelings between Jewish subgroups— tensions between the Ashkenazim and the Sephardim, and between the Reform and the Orthodox. At first my father said he would not go to the wedding if I got married in a Reform temple. He wanted an Orthodox rabbi. In order to please my father, I went to see his rabbi, who told me that if I got married in a Reform temple I would not be legally married according to Jewish law. I had hoped he would come to the temple and participate in the ceremony, but he absolutely refused. I was angered.

"Listen," I told him, "a piece of paper, or the synagogue, is not going to make our marriage better or worse. If there is a God, I am sure He doesn't plan to bring two people together and then spoil their marriage because they did not get married in an Orthodox synagogue."

When I saw my father the next day, I told him about my conversation with the rabbi. Sandy and I were not going to change our plans. "You have a choice," I said. "Either you come, or you are going to spoil it for everybody."

He backed down and agreed to attend the ceremony. My father, God bless him, was a very practical person. He knew, as the saying goes, "What is to God is to God, what is to people is to people." Sandy's little grandma, who was Orthodox and kept a kosher home, would advise him what food he could eat at the reception.

Our wedding date was set for December 18, 1955. During our five-month engagement, I was on the road a good deal. I would be gone for two weeks, and then back for a weekend. So the pressure of preparing for the wedding was tremendous. We would also talk to each other about what we wanted out of life. I wanted two children, whereas Sandy, an only child, wanted four or more. We wound up one night in such an argument that she accused me of hating children.

She offered to return the diamond ring I'd given her and was ready to call off the engagement. We were as different as two people could be. I knew what poverty is. I knew what it is to be hungry, to lose everything and start from the beginning. Sandy had led a protected life. Although her parents were not rich, she never knew what it was like to be hungry or to do without anything.

We had a difficult time finding mutual ground. Even our friends were different. Many of my friends were Sephardic, and she shared the Ashkenazi prejudice of the time that they were crude. My friends were also older and moved in different circles from her younger friends. But she was a good sport, and she learned to adapt.

The day before the wedding, I decided that instead of staying home, I would spend the night in a hotel. I stayed at the Olympic Hotel in Seattle, where the reception was to be held the next day. I got a little drunk all by myself, but it was fun. When I got up in the morning, I could not believe it. It was snowing hard. I had driven in this kind of weather in Idaho and Oregon, so I knew I could handle it. I had a huge breakfast and a shower and then went home. My father and my two younger brothers, Isaac and Mendel, were very excited, but nervous. They wondered if anybody would show up in all that snow. We lived on a little hill, but I assured them that I would get them to the temple. We made it, although we got stuck twice. Surprisingly, I think the only person we lost because of the snowstorm was Sandy's hairdresser.

Rabbi Raphael Levine, who married us, told us before the ceremony something I will never forget. "No matter how angry you may get with each other," he said, "if before you go to bed you can say to each other 'I'm sorry, I was wrong, please forgive me,' your marriage will last for many years." I still practice that. During the course of our marriage, his advice proved useful many times.

Needless to say, my life was now altered irrevocably. All of a sudden I had to think of another person. And many of the things that I was used to doing would have to change. During the High Holy Days, for example, I never drove a car. Sandy, however, belonged to the Reform temple and she was used to driving there. We decided that she would drive and I would ride as a passenger, but I knelt down on the floor of the car all the way there. I was not afraid of what God might do to me, but I was afraid that someone might see me in the car and might tell my father. I did not want to upset him.

Soon after we were married, Sandy decided she wanted to go to work. She got a job at Best's Apparel, which then sold women's clothing and later merged with Nordstrom. During the entire time that Sandy worked in that store, I never saw a paycheck, because they constantly had sales and offered discounts for the employees.

When we were in Moses Lake, on our first vacation, Sandy got pregnant. We were not planning to have a child so soon after our wedding. I told Sandy not to worry, she was not going to get pregnant. So much for my past experience!

At the time, we had lived in Shorewood Apartments on Mercer Island for almost a year, but because Sandy was pregnant, we started looking for a house. Like all young couples, we could not afford too much. Finally, right after Christmas that year, I remembered hearing about a place in Bellevue called Spiritwood. The real estate agent took us to see a half-finished house on a large corner lot. We just fell in love with it.

It had all the things that fit our needs at that time — a huge living room, two bathrooms, three bedrooms, a family room, and a garage. This was on a Sunday. On Monday, I signed the papers.

That night I could not sleep because it was the first time that I was going into debt. The house cost $17,250 with a small down payment. I bought the house on the G.I. Bill, and the interest that I was paying at that time was 4.5 percent. My monthly payments, with insurance and taxes and interest, came to about $105. But to me that was a lot of money. We moved into the house in February 1957.

Our first son did not come easy. The baby was due in April. I canceled my road trips. On May eighth I was drilling a stump so we could plant it with flowers when Sandy told me the doctor said it was time to go to the hospital. I almost drilled my own leg. After taking Sandy to the hospital, I called her mother and her aunt Jenny immediately. Sandy needed a cesarean, which would take about two hours. A couple of hours passed. No sign of Sandy or the baby. Two and a half hours, and then three hours. Still no nurse or doctor to tell me what was happening.

I began to think the worst. I saw someone being wheeled out of surgery and I thought it was Sandy, but it was not. I thought I was being punished for all the bad things that I had ever done. I was sure Sandy was dead, and I did not know what had happened to the baby. About four hours later the doctor finally came out and told me I was the father of a seven-and-a-half-pound baby boy.

This was the greatest, happiest, and most exciting moment in my life. I jumped up and kissed the doctor, and I ran and told Sandy's mother that she had a grandson. I was flying.

And May eighth was a historic date, as well. It had marked the end of Nazi Germany and of the war in Europe.

We knew that if we had a boy we would name him Robert, with a middle name beginning with "J" for Sandy's brother, Jackie, who passed away when he was just six.

Two months after Robert was born, Sandy announced to me that she was pregnant again. I thought this was impossible. How could she be? Nevertheless, she was, and I had to accept it.

It was not easy for me, but it was much harder for Sandy. I was not very much help to her because I was only in town two weeks out of every four. Nine months later Sandy had another cesarean. This time she gave birth to a baby girl, whom we named Deborah. We were thrilled. Just as we had hoped, a boy and a girl.

Three months after Debbie was born, Sandy was pregnant *again*. Now she was extremely upset. Needless to say, I was not very happy about it either, but I was not as upset as Sandy. The third pregnancy in such a short time created a strain on our marriage and on our budget, but it also made our marriage more solid because we had to depend more on each other for support.

Until June of 1955, I had been loose and free, living selfishly from day to day. Now my wife, before her twenty-second birthday, had given birth to our third child, Jeffrey. I surely did not expect all this responsibility. I was making a living, but that was just about it. Before I was married, I had a few thousand dollars in the bank and felt it was all the money I needed.

I remember one time after I had just come home from a sales trip. We were in bed and it was maybe eleven o'clock when I got a phone call from the police station. "We have a kid here who says you're his brother. His name is Mendel Friedman."

"What's the problem?" I asked.

"We found him at a high school dance," the officer said. "He had liquor on his breath and admitted to drinking beer. Will you please come and get him?"

Mendel was fourteen or fifteen at the time. I was angry, although I understood that the difficult circumstances of Mendel's early years had made it hard for him to adjust. Mother had passed away when he was barely nine years old.

I had no one to turn to for help except my wife. As a matter of fact, after about a year of marriage we went on a trip together, and one night in a tiny motel in Brooking, Oregon, I told my Sandy all the secrets of my past that I had kept to myself all these years. It was a confession of all my sins. No other soul knows all my secrets except my wife, and I told her all of this within the first year of our marriage. Perhaps it helped her to understand me better.

# The Arnie Apple Company,
# the World's Fair,
# and Family Life

ANDY THOUGHT I SHOULD GO INTO BUSINESS
for myself. I explained that I didn't have enough capital. But I
knew a guy in the fashion jewelry business named Arnie Apple
who had just split from working with his father.

"Why don't you ask him?" Sandy said.

"I don't think it would be right because he is friendly with my boss,
Mr. Klein." As a matter of fact, we were located in the same building. "If
I ask him, he might pass the word on to my boss and things wouldn't look
very good."

I had talked to Albert Klein about becoming a partner with him, but
his son Arthur was coming out of the army and would be joining the
business.

One day in November 1960, we were out of some fashion jewels we
needed before Christmas. I knew that Arnie Apple always had more
merchandise than he could sell, so I went to his office. He complained
about how hard he was working. As a joke, I told him he needed a partner.

"Would you be interested?" he asked.

"Under the right conditions, yes."

In March 1961 Arnie called, and we met at his home. After hours of talking, we decided to form a fifty-fifty partnership.

I came back and told my boss, Mr. Klein, of my opportunity to go into partnership with Arnie Apple. Mr. Klein offered me a ten percent share of his business, but I knew that I could never become equal partners. Albert Klein owned two-thirds of the business, and his brother Ludwig owned the other third. And Albert's son Arthur was about to join the business. When I suggested they sell me and Arthur a fifty-percent share, they turned me down flat. I finished the season with Mr. Klein, and then I began my partnership in the Arnie Apple Company.

I did not have enough capital, so I had to throw in my car, a beautiful copper Impala. I now needed a station wagon for business, and I had to borrow the money. I went to some of Sandy's relations with great hopes that they would lend me the money, but they all turned me down. Only my father and Sandy's parents, both of whom had little to spare, were willing to help. Her parents took out a second mortgage on their house in order to lend me some money. It was a great commitment for me to undertake this new business, and I was lucky to have the support of my wife and our small family.

We went ahead with our joint venture just about one year before Century 21 and the 1962 World's Fair in Seattle. We were fortunate to get the license to make souvenir jewelry and accessories for the upcoming event. This, in itself, was a tremendous boost for me and for the Arnie Apple Company. I worked two shifts during the fair and got maybe four hours of sleep. When I got up in the morning, after breakfast I would leave a tip on the table—I was too tired to remember whether I was at home or in a restaurant!

Our place of business above Nordstrom at Fifth and Pike in Seattle was too small to run two operations, so we maintained the Arnie Apple Company during the regular hours, and then we operated the newly formed souvenir company at night. We also had an additional partner in Michael Kent. He was the one responsible for getting the license to distribute World's Fair–logo jewelry at Century 21, the Space Needle, and the Monorail.

The World's Fair was a very exciting time for us, and we met some interesting people. One of them was a Frenchman named Albert Barcelone. He was one of our big customers at the fairgrounds, and he also bought fashion jewelry from us. He had a French boutique at the fair. One time a woman bought a necklace from him, assuming that it was French. When she examined it at home, she discovered "Made in Japan" inscribed on the clasp. She came to the boutique the next morning to complain. One of his clerks went over to Albert's office to explain the situation. Barcelone rushed out and kissed the woman's hand, saying, "Madame, how may I help you?"

"Look," she said. "You sold me French jewelry and this says 'Made in Japan'."

"Ah," he said. "Madame, this necklace is French but the clasp is Japanese. If you wish me to, I will be happy to change the clasp."

"No, no, everything is fine," she said.

We also had a customer whose place was called World Jewelry. When the Seattle World's Fair closed, he got the license for a Caribbean pavilion for the New York World's Fair and he wanted us to go in as his partners. Because the Seattle event had been so successful, naturally we wanted to provide souvenirs for the New York fair, but we could not get that license because of our being three thousand miles away.

The closing of the Seattle World's Fair was a tremendous letdown for us. At that time, the Arnie Apple Company had two salesmen in addition to the two of us. It was up to me to organize a larger sales force, since my responsibilities were for the outside while my partner's job was to be responsible for the inside. It did not quite work out that way, but that was the concept initially. Our first year in business, the Arnie Apple Company just about broke even, but we made a lot of money from the World's Fair. Our second year improved, and I was able to pay off some of the money I owed. By the fourth year, I had paid off all my creditors, including my parents-in-law and my father. Our sales force grew to four.

We were making more money, and we were working very hard. We saved a dollar wherever we could. For instance, we would have to go to Providence, Rhode Island, to buy new fashion merchandise. By flying via Canada we saved a hundred dollars each. We would drive up to Vancouver, B.C., leave the car at the airport, and then fly to Montreal at night and switch airplanes. From Montreal, we would catch a plane to New York and then to Providence and start working immediately. We would start at eight in the morning and work until ten o'clock at night.

All that I knew now was work. I worked many seven-day weeks. Even when I was on the road, I would take the customers out to dinner on a Sunday and then work with them that evening, or I would drive to the next city so I would be able to get a head start early in the morning. I did not know what it was to not work on a Saturday. When I was in town, I was in the office on Saturdays and Sundays. If I was on the road, I was working with customers on Saturdays.

I remember the first vacation Sandy and I had without the children. Our oldest child was nine years old, and my in-laws moved into the house to watch the kids. We flew to Hawaii. Sandy called home every day to ask how the children were. She was so concerned because she had never been away from them. We had a wonderful time together.

If anyone had told me after the war that one day I would be a devoted family man, I would have said, "Impossible. I'm not the type." My becoming domestic was like taking a wild horse and corralling him, then bridling him into a working horse. Who was responsible for turning this stallion into a working horse? My wife.

One of the more difficult periods of our family life was when my daughter Deborah injured herself. She was on an outing with a young women's group. As she was attempting to get out of a canoe, she stepped on some driftwood and punctured her foot. This turned into a nightmare and an ordeal that has left her in pain to this day. During Robert's bar mitzvah, Debbie was in a cast in a wheelchair. She has had many surgeries since that incident.

In those days, we did not think of suing doctors for incompetence, but today there would be no question about it. In my opinion, the camp counselors and the doctor were terribly, terribly negligent.

I REMEMBER OUR first large contribution to a charitable organization, the Kline Galland Home, a nursing home for the elderly. I originally made a pledge of two hundred fifty dollars to be paid off over a five-year period. I received a phone call from Sol Esfeld, a pillar of the Seattle community, and he persuaded me to raise my pledge to five hundred dollars. That was a lot of money for me, because I was still new in business. I came home that night and told Sandy.

"How could you?" she asked me. "We owe everybody so much money and we need all these things in the house, and yet you went ahead

and made a pledge for five hundred dollars. That's a hundred dollars a
year that you are giving away."

"Honey," I said. "We will make it."

I use this story today many times when I solicit money for different
organizations and causes. Sure it was lots of money at that time, but I
paid it off and was fortunate enough to make more money and make
larger and larger contributions to many, many good causes in the future.
It is good to give. I have been on both sides. I have been on the receiving
end, and believe me, it is very demeaning. I always felt kind of guilty, but
it is so much more rewarding when you are able to give to good causes
with your time and your financial help. I've learned over the years that
it's especially fulfilling to be able to give without expecting a thank you.
The hardest part is deciding how much to give to a charity. Once you have
made the pledge of a sum, the payment is much easier, and the more
you give, the better you feel about it.

I STILL BORE scars from World War II, both emotional and men-
tal. The Korean War did not help me either. However, in the 1960s and
1970s, the new upheaval caused by the Vietnam War created a different
generation, a different culture. My brother Mendel became a member
of this counterculture. I don't know how I would have reacted if I had
grown up in America at that time.

Mendel had served in the air force, and when he came out of the
military he seemed fine. Then he went to college, and all hell broke loose
in his mind. Whatever money he had saved from the air force, he gave
to a commune. He no longer seemed to have a mind of his own, and this
hurt me. My children loved Mendel and they looked up to him for guid-
ance, but I did not like his influence. He had been on drugs and he struck
me as a misfit. I had to tell him either to shape up or to stop coming over
to our house. I didn't want to see him again if he was unwilling to change.
We both cried because it was a very sad and painful decision. Sandy dis-
agreed with me.

I felt that Mendel would eventually come to his senses. In his failure, I felt that I had failed him. By not seeing him, I thought that I would
lessen my pain. Even though I didn't see him for about two years, I did
keep track of him through his friends. Sandy did see him, which was fine

with me. I had no objections to that. At times I felt a very heavy load on my shoulders, raising three children of my own and worrying about my brother. I was terrified that my daughter would lose her foot and leg. I felt that I had failed my youngest brother, because I was the eldest brother and was supposed to take care of him. I knew he was hurting and I felt helpless.

# Israel
# and Other
# Travels

I SRAEL'S WINNING OF THE SIX DAYS' WAR IN
1967 reinstated my sense of pride in being a Jew. I had always felt
saddened, even revolted, by what I perceived to be a failure of the
Jewish leadership for not fighting back against the Germans. I knew that
fighting would have been suicidal, but I always felt we would have
gained some dignity by doing so. Here and there Jewish guerrillas fought
back. The Warsaw Ghetto uprising, of course, was a moment all survivors are proud of. And had there been support of Jewish fighters by local populations, say, in the Ukraine, perhaps things might have turned
out differently.

I had always identified with the image of the Jewish fighter. After the
liberation, when I came to Poland, I immediately joined Hashomer
Hatzeir, because a former member, Mordechai Anielewicz, was also one
of the leaders of the Warsaw Ghetto uprising. Now Israel's victories made
me feel very good. I became a strong financial supporter of Israel.

Soon after the Six Days' War, I went on a Jewish Federation mission
to Israel so that I could see the needs of the country directly. This was
the first time I went to a foreign country without my wife, but I did prom-

ise her that we would make this trip with the family at a later date. Every year up to that point we had traveled together to different regions of the United States.

Everyone on the El Al flight was excited by the prospect of visiting Israel at this time, and I stayed up all night in anticipation. I kissed the soil when I arrived. No one can describe my feelings those first few days. I was proud to be in the majority.

I looked forward to meeting my uncle Salomon, my father's youngest brother. I had always felt close to him, although I had not seen or heard from him for over thirty years. His first wife and their daughter had been killed by the Germans, and now he was remarried and had a son.

Our group stayed in the Hilton Hotel in Tel Aviv. My uncle didn't live very far away, maybe an hour. I called him immediately and he told me to get some sleep. I took a hot shower and I dozed a little, but I was too anxious to really fall asleep. The last time I had seen Salomon was in 1938, and now it was 1970.

I was waiting anxiously for him when the phone rang. He was calling from the lobby of the hotel, with my aunt and cousin. They were coming up to see me. I walked out of my room into the hallway. When they stepped out of the elevator, I couldn't believe my eyes. What a moment. I recognized Uncle Salomon immediately. His hair was now gray, but he wore the same warm smile. I ran to him, and we embraced each other.

We sure did a lot of talking about the past. I learned that when Uncle Salomon was drafted into the Russian army in 1940, he was just a recruit. Five years later he was discharged as a captain. He almost died in 1945 when he was wounded near Berlin. That was when we lost all contact with him, because he spent many months in a hospital. On his discharge in 1946, he was all alone in the city of Lvov, his wife and daughter and most of his relatives murdered by the Nazis. He had lost all contact with us and Cousin Pepe.

He met Nina in Lvov. She was a Jew from what was then called Leningrad. Nina and my uncle met because they were working for the same government cooperative, she as an accountant and my uncle as a purchasing agent. She was much younger than Salomon. After a brief courtship, they were married, and they later had a son named Chaim.

After we settled in America, my father felt that his brother Salomon was still alive. So he kept writing letters to some of the Ukrainian people who knew his family in Russia. But he heard nothing. In 1957 he was awakened in the middle of the night by a telephone call. He said "wrong number" and hung up. Two hours later, the phone rang again. This time my father was really cross and said, "Stop harassing me or I'll call the police!" But the operator said this was Poland calling and that his brother Salomon wanted to talk to him. Salomon had managed to leave Russia with his family for what was officially only a visit to Poland. But he did not plan to return to Russia. We tried right away to bring him to America, but it was taking too long. Time was running out. Salomon went to the Israel embassy in Poland and told them of his problem. Within the week, he and his family were on a plane to Israel.

OUR GROUP WAS SCHEDULED to see Israel's achievements and learn of its needs. We rose early each morning, ate a quick breakfast in the hotel dining room, and were on the bus by 6:30 a.m. The trip to the Suez Canal was most memorable. We first took an airplane and flew from Tel Aviv to a base in the Sinai, where they demonstrated some tanks for us. From there, we mounted buses for the Suez. The guides were two beautiful sabra girls and they sang Hebrew songs for us. I was in seventh heaven: I was so proud of the Jewish people.

I saw Jewish farmers, truckdrivers, garbagemen, and bricklayers. A country was being built. When we arrived at the Suez Canal, I climbed to the top of a bunker and could look down to where the Egyptians had hidden. The canal was so narrow that we could almost throw a rock across.

We came back that evening to Tel Aviv. I could not sleep. I was so excited that I walked out of the hotel. Two women approached me with a proposition to have sex. I was shocked and could not believe it. I had an image of everybody being so pure. I forgot that the Israelis were also human. It was like finding out that your mother is a prostitute. I was so naïve. For some reason, I expected everyone in Israel to be above such behavior.

We also went to Yad VaShem, which is the memorial for the six million Jews who perished in the Holocaust. I had a very difficult time there. I wanted to get out, but they had closed the door behind our group for a special memorial service. A cantor was chanting. I can't describe the feeling that I had. It was the first time that I was faced again with the horror of the Holocaust. That night I had terrible nightmares and they continued for about two or three weeks afterwards.

I always wear a gold chain around my neck with the Star of David inscribed with the symbolic shield of the twelve tribes of Israel. I want people to know who I am wherever I go, and whenever I can, I always leave my shirt open. Sometimes it is an advantage, sometimes not. But I feel that I have to wear the Star of David because of the Holocaust. As a survivor, I feel I have the right to wear it no matter what the consequences. I am happy to tell the world today that I'm a Jew.

I was never so proud to call myself a Jew as I was after that trip. It was almost a royal trip because it was sponsored by the Israel military and by the government, so we got to see what the average tourist does not get to see.

WHEN I RETURNED to the United States, I continued to work hard at our business. We had eight salesmen now, covering the western states, and we were making good money. Before I came to America, I had the impression that in America money fell from the sky. What a surprise to learn that you actually had to work for it. There is no other country in the world that offers people the opportunities that America does. I wished many times that my mother could still be alive to see what I was able to accomplish here. She, more than my father, was responsible for getting me to come to America. I always felt she was cheated from seeing her children's successes.

Many people think that by waiting, things will fall properly into place. I've learned that it does not happen that way. If you want to achieve your goals, you have to work for them.

I now wanted to return to my roots in Poland. When I started to make the arrangements, my father became very nervous. He was afraid for me to return to the Ukraine. He was especially concerned about the Symchucks. He had given them a pledge that he would not reveal or publish their names, because they were afraid in those years immediately following the war that people in their own village would kill them.

As it turned out, I could not get a visa to the city of Brody. I could go to Moscow and to Leningrad, but not to Brody, which was where I wanted to go. I canceled my plans. In 1977 we flew to London instead, where we did the usual tourist things—Buckingham Palace, the Royal Ballet, the theater. After two weeks, I was excited to fly to Salzburg, my old stamping grounds. I had been there after the war at least three or four times a month between 1946 and 1949.

Sandy and I stayed in a hotel on the Danube River. From our room we had a view of a castle and the Winkler Café, one of my favorite places when I lived in Austria. From there we drove through the Alps and visited Bad Ischl, where I had spent a week in a hotel after the war. I could not believe how the town had shrunk. The whole park had changed; it was very small. Bad Ischl had been the summer home of Emperor Franz Josef. It was where the declaration had been signed to begin World War I.

I played chess on the grounds of the park, but I was disappointed that it was not as it had been when I left the country. We also went to the salt mines, and that was quite an experience for both of us. When I lived in Austria after the war, I felt two feet taller than the Austrians. When I came back this time, the Austrians wanted to give me the impression that they were head and shoulders above me.

We next visited Linz, Austria, where I had spent about three years after the war. Many of the restaurants and stores I had frequented were gone, replaced by new shops or torn down. The D.P. camp of Ebelsberg where I had lived was now an Austrian army barracks, and I was not allowed to enter. We were not even permitted to take pictures of the barracks.

We also visited the Mauthausen concentration camp, which had been in the Russian zone about five miles from Linz. I had never been there during the war or after. Who in their right mind would have wanted to? But now Sandy thought we should see it. I was very apprehensive. When we arrived at the camp at 4:30 p.m. it was closed. This gave me a chance to prepare myself psychologically. I had convinced myself before going to sleep that this was the past, and I was living in the present. I knew what I would see, whereas Sandy was totally unprepared for what we encountered when we entered the camp the next day. It was far worse than any description in a book.

After we walked through the first barracks, Sandy said that she had seen enough. She did not want to go any farther. She could smell death. I felt that she was cheating herself from experiencing what the victims had had to go through. In a way, I forced her to continue so that she could really see the horrors of the camp. After we saw the ovens, she hardly spoke a word. She was in pain. Later, on our way back to Linz, she said to me that all Americans, all human beings, should see for themselves what had happened there. Perhaps then hatred, racism, bigotry would cease. Days later she claimed that she could still smell death and hear the screams of the people. Sandy accused me of wanting her to feel my pain. This was not what I had in mind. I just wanted her to know something of the pain the victims had experienced.

On our way from Linz to Vienna, we stopped in an old monastery where there was a wonderful art collection. Much of it had been hidden in salt mines during the war. I found Vienna to be more anti-Semitic than Salzburg or Linz. We walked into an antique store and saw a beautiful clock that we both fell in love with. We wanted to take it back with us.

The owner looked at me and said, "Beautiful things like this should not leave Austria."

"I want to buy it," I said. "It doesn't belong to your country. It was probably taken from a Jewish family."

"If you want it, take it out the way it is. I do not wrap or pack my clocks," she said. The clock was thirty inches high and maybe eighteen inches wide.

"I cannot take it that way," I said.

"But that is how my customers take them," she said.

I stormed out of her store, slamming the door behind me. I hoped the clock would break and become worthless to this arrogant woman. When we returned to Seattle, I decided not to visit Europe again for quite some time.

# Family
# News

O UR CHILDREN WERE GROWING UP. MY DAUGH-
ter Debbie was seriously dating Larry Benezra, the son of
Joyce and Ray Benezra, whose wedding reception I crashed
the night I met Sandy. We liked Larry a lot. He was very much like me
in character—very tense and direct. He was the type of a guy that if you
dropped him in the middle of the ocean, he would find a way to survive.

When Debbie and Larry told us they were in love and planned to
get married, we were very happy. Not only did we feel that Larry was a
very capable and personable guy who would take good care of our daughter, but we knew the family, and we were friends. We knew the kind of
home that Larry came from. We knew his grandparents.

They were married on December 18, 1977, on our twenty-second
wedding anniversary. The wedding took place at Temple de Hirsch Sinai,
and the reception was held at the Olympic Hotel. Nearly four hundred
people attended, and I must say it was one of the most beautiful weddings
given in Seattle at that time. No money was spared.

My uncle Salomon and his wife Nina came from Israel for the wedding, which made the event so much more meaningful. The only prob-

lem was that it all went by so fast. Before I knew it my daughter was coming to me to say good-bye. That really broke me up. Suddenly I did not like Larry. I felt he was taking my daughter away. I cried all the way home. My father had left earlier.

By the time I got home, I was still crying, and my dad was still up. It was about three-thirty in the morning. He hit the table with his hand and said, "What the hell are you crying about? She married a nice Jewish boy from a nice family, and what is your complaint?"

"Dad," I said. "You would never understand because you never had a daughter. It is one thing to have a son leave, but it is another thing entirely to let go of your daughter."

In 1980 Debbie informed us that she was pregnant. We were all very excited, but this was especially meaningful to me. How lucky I felt to be alive. Once I did not care if the Germans killed me just so long as I had a full stomach. Now I cried from happiness when I learned that I would become a grandfather. I could not wait until our first grandchild was born.

For the first year, we saw Anthony at least once a week. We were not the type of in-laws to drop in. We would always call and ask first. But when Anthony was born, we visited Debbie and her husband constantly. This was one of the most rewarding periods of my life. We took picture after picture of Anthony.

MY BROTHER ISAAC, who was married now and had two sons of his own, became a very good court reporter. The judges often encouraged him to go to law school. Finally, he decided to apply, but he did not have a college degree. In California, there are junior bar exams for those without a college degree. Isaac took the junior bar exam, passed it, and went to law school at night, continuing to work as a court reporter during the day. He eventually graduated with honors and passed his bar exam on the first try. He's now a very successful attorney practicing in California.

I think back to our time in hiding when he would gesture silently in front of a chimney. He would stand there for hours. Now he gestures in front of a judge and wins cases for his clients, but during our captivity he did this just to pass the time.

Our father moved to Los Angeles because the climate was warmer. He had hoped to buy a house where he and Isaac's family could live together. That was his Old World idea, but he learned quickly that in

America, children live independently of their parents. Besides, he was too stubborn and independent himself to accommodate others. He ate kosher food, while they did not. There were just too many differences to make such a situation work. So he rented a duplex in the Fairfax district of Los Angeles, and he lived there happily. Every time we went to Los Angeles, we would visit him and he would enjoy cooking for us, making his European dishes, especially potato pancakes, which I dearly loved.

Father got a job with a janitorial company when he moved to Los Angeles, and he finally retired after working as a handyman for the Beverly Hills Hotel. As a matter of fact, my brothers and I were concerned. What will Father do with himself? But our father was a very organized person. It so happened that his second wife developed Alzheimer's disease, and that kept him very busy after he retired. His wife passed away about eighteen months after his retirement, but by that time he had a routine.

He didn't sleep much at night. He would do his chores in the early morning, or go to the temple and say his prayers, or say them at home very early. Then he would go off and do some shopping. He was systematic. He liked to go to the park early and play cards with his friends. He was never an idle person. He had a vegetable garden in his back yard, and he made his own wines. They were very good.

I always enjoyed visiting with my father because he liked to hear about my business success. He was especially fond of Sandy, who he felt was good for me. He loved to play gin rummy, but he hated to lose. The Friedmans are all very poor losers. No matter what game my brothers and I play, we have to be winners. Our father must have instilled in us a competitive drive.

My brother Mendel, after going through many years of difficult times in his life searching for a place in the American society, finally settled his differences with me. I helped him buy a house, which he then remodeled. He did an excellent job of fixing it up. He entered the real estate business and he made a success of himself, which makes me very happy.

IN APRIL 1983, WHEN I was in Providence, Rhode Island, I got a call from my brother Isaac that our father had died. It was a terrible shock to me, because I had seen Father just one week before in Los Angeles. Generally, when we greeted each other, it was a handshake and a hug, but the last time I saw him we kissed each other. I thought that perhaps he had some intuition that he was going to die. He died sitting in his chair reading his newspaper. He just went to sleep. That was it. He never wanted to be placed in a home for the elderly. He had seen many of his friends in hospitals and nursing homes, and he did not want to go that way. We promised him that we would not let this happen, that we would hire a nurse for him twenty-four hours a day. It was a blessing for him to die the way he did.

My mother had died during Passover, and now my father died during Passover, too. Because it was Eastertime, it was very difficult to get airline tickets to Los Angeles. We had been scheduled to go from Providence to Washington, D.C., for the first gathering of the Holocaust survivors in the United States. Instead, in the middle of the night I made our travel arrangements to Los Angeles, and the next morning I flew out.

The entire family met in Los Angeles for the funeral. Father, we learned, had made all the arrangements — the land, the cemetery. He had paid for everything in advance, which upset my brothers and me. The arrangements followed Orthodox Jewish law and seemed austere and cold to us.

I was deeply hurt that my father did not trust us to take care of him, that he felt he had to do everything himself. Even as I sit here now and write this, I feel hurt that he had so little faith in me to take care of him properly. The last time I was with him he had few complaints. He was always happy. If I complained about something he would tell me that I should be content.

Now he was gone. He was so independent that I felt cheated because he never gave me the pleasure of making life easier for him. For example, when we were in China, we bought him a beautiful cashmere sweater because he was always cold. My father gave the sweater to my son. He felt it was too good for himself. Then my daughter bought him a beautiful sweater for one of his birthdays and she told him that he could not return this one, that he should wear it and enjoy it. My father kept it, but he never wore it. He showed it to his landlord and said, "Look what my granddaughter bought me. It's beautiful, but where can I wear it? It's a shame she wasted this money." When Father died, his landlord

The Great Synagogue in Brody, Poland, before World War II

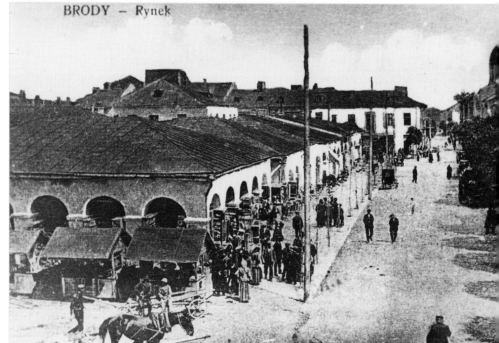

BRODY — Rynek

(*Facing page, top*) The Brody railway terminal and the road into Brody

(*Facing page, bottom*) Market Street in Brody in the 1930s

The Brody Gymnasium (secondary school) in pre-war days.
After the occupation, Jewish children were no longer
permitted to attend this school.

Here I am, in my white shirt and knickers, with my cousins Anschul and Yite Strouse. The year was 1936. My cousin Pepe was also in the photo, but she cut herself out before she gave it to me. Pepe was the only one of my father's relatives to survive the Nazi occupation.

Klara Friedman with her granddaughter Yite in 1938. In 1942
my grandmother tried to save her grandson Anschul, but Nazi soldiers
shot him and burned down her house with her inside it.

The barn in Suchowola where Mrs. Maria Bazalchik
hid my father for eighteen months

My cousin Pepe and her husband Joseph in 1945. Pepe escaped from
the pogrom at Zlotchiw during the first week of the Nazi occupation.
She was hidden till war's end by the family of a Ukrainian priest.

At age seventeen, in the town of Gliwice, Silesia. The year was 1945.

In Enns, Austria, in 1947

With my mother and father in Enns, 1947

My permit to drive a truck. Linz, Austria, 1947

At twenty, the man about town. Linz, 1948

Fire drill aboard the *General Sturgess,* on the way
to the United States. November 1949

Ivan and Marie Symchuck with one of their granddaughters.
For a year and a half during the occupation, the Symchucks hid my
mother, my brother, our teacher, and me in the crawl space below
the roof of their house. This picture was taken during the 1950s.

Julia Symchuck (*right*) with her mother and her niece
and nephew during the 1950s

(*Facing page, top*) My brother Isaac, who survived with me. Seattle, 1952

(*Facing page, bottom*) During my military tour of duty. Sasebo, Japan, 1952

My uncle Salomon survived in the Russian army. His wife and daughter were killed during the occupation. He is shown here in 1959 with his second wife, Nina, and their son Chaim.

The ruins of the Great Synagogue. Brody, 1988

The Great Synagogue. 1988

A set of carved doors, originally from the Great Synagogue at Brody,
now housed in the Jewish Museum in Paris, France

A monument to Brody in the Holocaust cemetery in Israel

With Julia Symchuck on her visit to Seattle in July 1989. Photograph
by Scott Eklund. Courtesy of the Bellevue *Journal American*

(*Facing page, top*) Governor Booth Gardner honoring Julia Symchuck
during her Seattle visit. (*From left to right*) interpreter Mr. Silverman,
Julia Symchuck, my wife Sandy, Governor Booth Gardner, myself,
and my granddaughter Selena Benezra. July 1989

(*Facing page, bottom*) With Pope John Paul II, at the Yom Hashoah
(Day of Remembrance) ceremonies at the Vatican in April 1994.
A group of Holocaust survivors representing twelve countries were invited
to take part in this first Vatican commemoration of the Shoah.
For the first time within the Vatican, the Kol Nidre was sung and
a kaddish was chanted.

Our family in 1998. (*Front row, left to right*) Jonathan Friedman; Selena, Jeremy, and Anthony Benezra; Joshua Friedman; Sandra Friedman. (*Back row, left to right*) Jeff Friedman, holding his son Jordan; Robin Friedman; Larry and Deborah Benezra; Robert Friedman; and myself called us and said he only wanted one thing of my father's — and that was the sweater that our daughter had sent him.

Father was a proud man. I loved him. I never had the opportunity to say that to him. I respected him, but I never said *thank you* while he was alive. I knew he was smart, but I never gave him the credit while he was alive. I did not realize how fortunate I was to have his counsel even though I did not always hear him. I guess I will always carry some of the pain and hurt with me for the rest of my life because I did not say *thanks* while he was here.

I owe much of my success to my father. If he had not had the wisdom to hide us from the Nazis, I would not be here to tell this story. If, after liberation, my father had not enlisted in the Polish army and later forced us to leave Russia for Poland, I would not have been able to write this. If in 1946, after the war, my father had not seen the handwriting on the wall as far as Jews were concerned in Poland, and if he had not taken us then to Austria, I would not be here today. If my father had not forced me to leave Austria to come to America, I definitely would not have prospered as I have. America presented me with opportunities I would not have had otherwise.

My father finished only three grades of regular school. He never went beyond that in formal education. He was a self-taught man. I have had a little more education than my father, but nothing to compare with the educations of the people I have had to deal with in my life. I owe much of my success to him.

THE YEAR 1985 was eventful for our family. Rob's wife, Lynn, whom he had married on January 7, 1984, gave birth to a son who was named Joshua Louis Friedman, the first male grandchild to carry my name.

Jeff became a doctor in June 1985. I was thrilled to see him at the podium in an auditorium of one of the country's most prestigious hospitals — Mt. Sinai in New York. I felt as if I were the one graduating and was very proud of my youngest son's achievement.

On September 30, 1985, Debbie had a daughter, my first granddaughter. Sandy and I both wanted a girl after three grandsons.

In January 1986, Jeff announced his engagement to Robin Cohen of

New York. They planned to be married in August in New York. The whole family, including my brother Mendel, my brother Isaac and his wife, and Sandy's father, flew east for the wedding. As Jeff was the last child to be married, we wanted the entire family to be there.

My daughter-in-law has excellent taste. The wedding could not have been nicer if the Queen of England had given it.

The year 1987 proved to be another busy one for my family. For the first time, all my children were within minutes of my house instead of hours by air. In July, Jeff came back to Seattle with his wife. After ten years away, he was home and was hoping for a permanent residence. He was here for two years of research at the University of Washington and hoped eventually to get into a program for orthopedic surgery. When Jeff had turned eighteen, I'd encouraged him to go away to college. There was no question in my mind that Jeff, of my three children, was probably the most capable of taking care of himself. I later discovered that he missed the closeness of being part of the family. I also somewhat regretted encouraging him to pursue a medical career. If I had known the pain and hard work that it entailed, I probably would have encouraged him to get into a fine business school. This would have taken a much shorter time, and he would have attained success sooner. But to refugees who survived the Holocaust, a doctor in the family has a special meaning. For me, to have a child become a doctor was a way to give something to future society. If I had suggested business school, however, Jeff would probably have turned me down. Since the time when he was little, he was committed to the profession of healing other people.

In the middle of the year 1988, we were saddened by the divorce of Robert and Lynn. I took it very personally. As a survivor, I saw it as my own failure as well as Rob's and Lynn's. But I am very happy to say that our grandson Joshua is still close to us.

# A Gathering
# of Survivors

N APRIL 1983 WE WENT TO THE FIRST AMER-
ican gathering of Jewish Holocaust survivors, in Washington, D.C.
I was very nervous on my way there, wondering if I would run into
somebody that I knew in those days after the war. I kept thinking, how
will I recognize people that I knew thirty or forty years ago? How will
they look today?

After we had registered at the meeting, events moved very quickly.
President Reagan was to address us in the convention center, and you
had to have tickets to get into this hall. There was a mix-up, and somehow I received tickets for the VIP section. We were fifteen rows from the
president of the United States. There were approximately fifteen thousand people in attendance. We had to go through tough security to get
into the hall. It was a very emotional time for me. I felt extremely vulner-
able as I listened to the president speak. The entire time I was a bundle
of nerves. Before going to bed each night, I had to have a drink.

When I was in hiding in the hayloft, if somebody had told me that
one day I would be in America, I would have said that person was crazy.
All I wanted was a decent meal. I didn't care what else happened to me.

But going to America, that was like going to the moon. Sitting up in the loft with a straw roof in our little village, I had never seen a building more than five stories high. Relatives used to send us postcards from New York with those tall buildings pictured on them, and it always amazed me. I used to wonder what happened when it was cloudy. Did the floors extend above the clouds? Could people see the top side of clouds from their windows? If someone had told me that first day in Boston when I got off the boat that one day I would be sitting a short distance from the president of the United States, I would have said that person was crazy also. Never in my wildest dreams could I have visualized such grandeur.

I felt very gratified, but I also realized that I would have to do something more than just feel gratified. I promised myself that in the future I would give more of myself to those who had died, who did not escape the concentration camps. Years before, a group had been organized in Seattle to build a monument in memory of the Holocaust. It was built at the Jewish Community Center on Mercer Island, and I made a generous contribution toward it. But I did not want to have any part of it because I wanted to forget my past. After listening to the president and other speakers, I changed my mind.

I realized that I have a duty because I am a survivor. I have a duty to help the future generations remember those people who passed away, that it was not all in vain. I have a duty because I am alive and because I am a witness to what happened. I realized that I must tell the true story, to respond to untruths or to those who deny the Holocaust ever happened. I realized that I have a purpose in life, that God saved me for a reason. I also discovered that much of the guilt I carried around inside me was because of not wanting to talk about my past.

The next morning, we went back to the meeting place. Signs were posted there, with messages: Do you know of such and such a person? or, If you are from the city of Lodz, please identify yourself in this section. People would go to a microphone and announce, "I am from so-and-so, and if you are from so-and-so, please come." I too went up to the microphone and said, "I am from Brody, and anyone here from Brody please identify yourself. My name is Henry Friedman. I would like to meet you." I waited for a while and then a lady came over and we embraced each other.

"I am not from Brody," she said, "but my husband is, and I know some people who are from Brody. If you give me your address, I will get you in touch with those people." I was very excited and very nervous.

We did meet those former residents of Brody on our next trip to New York, two months later. They gave me the name of someone I had known in Brody. We were the only two young guys who survived out of thousands of young people. I was very eager to meet anyone who survived the same time and place as I did. I had his father's phone number and I called him. The father, like most foreigners who had gone through what we had, was suspicious. He did not remember me, but I explained who I was. He took my number down and gave it to his son Moses, who did call me.

We met in New York. We had known each other when he was eighteen years old. Now it was forty years later. I was in my room in the Hotel St. Moritz, waiting anxiously, trying to visualize how he would look. Finally I got a call that he was downstairs in the lobby waiting for me. When I came down, he had a smile on his face that had not changed. Everything else about him had changed. He was heavier. He still had a full head of hair, but now it was gray.

We spent hours talking. It was obvious that he had lived a tougher life than I had. He had lived in Israel, in England, and now in America. I was hoping to see him again on our next trip, but he did not respond to my calls. I assume he was too uncomfortable to invite me to his home. He did not want to go into the past or to continue our relationship.

At the gathering of survivors in Washington, D.C., I ran into Sidney Wapner, whom I knew when I first arrived in Seattle. When I was in the army, Sidney moved into our home and lived with my family for a while. Now, we both had sons who had graduated from Brandeis. Sidney was born in Bialystok, and he had been in Auschwitz. He told us that CBS interviewed him about his life. He had recently met up with a gentleman who had helped him survive in the concentration camp.

THE PROCESS OF MEETING fellow survivors put my nerves on edge. It was painful. When you cut your finger it hurts, but then you forget about it. But you can't forget your history, as hard as you may try. That is what happened to me. We witnessed Jewish plays performed in

Yiddish by survivors which brought back memories. Children of survivors sang for our entertainment. I remember listening to the children of survivors who said they felt cheated by their parents because their parents tried to spare them from the painful stories.

I realized that I had nothing to be ashamed of, that I should not have any guilt feelings about my past. I survived to contribute. I had served in the United States Army, and with the help of my wife, I had raised a family I was very proud of.

But I realized that I had to do more than just be a survivor. I had to tell my story and tell what had happened to me. At that point in my life, I employed about twenty-five people. After Washington, D.C., I realized that I had to do more than I had done in the past. My father's death strengthened this feeling. He had never spoken of his past. My brother, who is a very good attorney and who gives legal advice to Holocaust survivors, wants to forget and is unable to talk about the past. I felt that I had to do something.

Immediately I started to explore the possibility of building a Holocaust center in Seattle. I knew that a Holocaust museum was to be built in Washington, D.C. — the cornerstone had been laid when we were there — but how many people from the Northwest would be able to travel to that museum? Very few. So I felt an obligation. I met with the Jewish leadership in Seattle on this project, and at that time I met with a leading business person who knew the Seattle community. He asked me how much money it would take. I told him approximately $750,000 to $1,000,000, provided we could get the building for free. "Before you undertake this," he said, "see if you can raise two-thirds of the amount."

I started to solicit pledges. I became very disappointed because a lot of prominent people refused to help. A Holocaust museum was not a priority for them. I was upset and I lost many nights of sleep. The person I had envisioned to head the fund-raising drive turned me down. This hurt a lot. His father had brought him to the United States when he was very young. "I am sick and tired of hearing about the Holocaust," he said. "Enough is enough. Let's forget about the past."

There was talk in Seattle of converting the old Temple de Hirsch Sinai sanctuary into a Jewish museum. I got involved because I felt that I could not raise enough funds for the Holocaust museum by myself. What I needed was a base and an organization to work from. I was also elected vice president of the Washington Jewish Historical Society, another vehicle that helped me accomplish some of my ideas. I knew that I had a mission. I felt that so far I had not done enough, that I would have to do more for the people who could not tell their own stories of the Holocaust.

# India

I N   M Y   W O R L D   T R A V E L S ,   O N E   T R I P   T H A T   S T A N D S
out in my mind is our journey to India in October 1984. For me,
what happened there was like a replay of the past in a different setting, and I was not a bystander.

By the time we arrived in New Delhi, we had visited Bombay,
Aurangabad, Srinagar, Udaipur, and Jaipur. We had found the people of
India to be very interesting, with a rich and ancient history, and with
Moors, Buddhists, Hindus and other religious groups seemingly inter-
acting in a tolerant and easy-going way. Even in Srinagar, a Kashmir state
in which most people were Moslems and not really happy to be part of
India, there was no violence. Most of the jewelry trade was controlled by
Moslems, with whom we had fun, as we had fun with the Hindus. On the
night of our arrival in New Delhi, we met a group of Sikhs in a restaurant, and we partied with them.

The next day in New Delhi we toured the city and visited the tomb
and former home of Mahatma Gandhi. We also went to a jewelry whole-
saler. As they were showing me stones, I noticed all around me that
people were talking in hushed whispers. Their faces had turned ashen.

"What's the matter?" I asked the man who was helping me.

"Mrs. Gandhi has been shot," he said.

"I don't believe that!" I replied.

We left immediately. I was in no mood to make a purchase. We were taken back to our hotel, and in the lobby I encountered the minister of tourism, who confirmed that the prime minister had indeed been assassinated. "She is dead," he said, "and there may be war with Pakistan. Her death is Pakistan's fault."

What happened next was madness and mass hysteria. Two Sikhs who were part of Mrs. Gandhi's own security guard were the assassins, and people throughout the country immediately decided that all Sikhs were guilty. Women, children, old men — all had to be punished with death.

I was in shock. I wondered how we would leave the country, nervous that we would be caught in a war zone. Our guide picked us up, and we kept to our schedule of touring New Delhi. Everywhere in the streets we could see that Sikhs were being harassed. A Sikh on a motorcycle in front of us was hit by a car. He was deliberately hit. We could not believe our eyes; no one stopped to help him. As the day progressed, we witnessed more hostilities. I was terribly upset, especially since up until now I had seen what I thought was tolerance between the different religious and ethnic groups.

By late afternoon we had decided to head back to our hotel but got stuck in traffic. I saw a lot of military personnel on the road and all over the area. I thrust my video camera out the window so I would be ready to take pictures. An officer came by and told me to put the camera away, because a soldier could mistake the camera for some kind of weapon. I asked him what was happening.

"The president of India is coming from the airport," he said. "That is the reason you are caught in traffic. Close your window and don't stick anything outside the car, because the soldiers are ready to shoot at anything that is suspicious."

"Yes, sir," I said.

A few minutes later we saw the caravan coming. Eventually, we made it back to our hotel. Sandy was very nervous. I tried to assure her that we were well protected. There were soldiers all around the hotel and grounds. Besides, we were very close to the airport, which was only about twenty minutes from the hotel. We noticed that both large and small tour groups were leaving the hotel. There was a feeling of panic in the air. We were scheduled to leave the next day. Despite our concern, we decided to go outside and walk the streets.

When we dined that night in the hotel dining room, through the windows we could see fires burning in New Delhi. We only discovered later how many Sikhs had been killed and how extensive was the damage.

Many of the waiters in the hotel restaurant were Sikhs. They were very frightened, and I could feel their pain and anxiety. It was clearly uncomfortable for them to be waiting on us while their homes were being burned in neighborhoods not far from the hotel. I felt very saddened by the events of the day and what I saw all around me. I remembered when we were in hiding and, through a hole in the side of the barn, I could see Polish farmers being thrown into the fire and burned to death by the Ukrainians. These Sikhs were innocent people being killed indiscriminately by their own countrymen.

I did not sleep very well that night. Fortunately, our guide picked us up early the next morning, and we made it to the airport without incident. We caught our plane and arrived in Agra very early in the morning.

As we were driving to our hotel from the airport, we saw a mob in front of us that was stopping cars. This was the first time I was frightened for our safety. I always felt that I could talk myself out of difficult situations, but I did not know how I could manage with a mob. The driver told us not to worry. Teenagers stopped our car and demanded to know if we were hiding any Sikhs. They let us pass when they could see for themselves that we were hiding no one.

Our guide had an employee who was a Sikh, and he asked us if we would mind if he stopped at his office to warn this fellow not to leave because it wouldn't be safe for him out on the street. We readily agreed.

Next day we left for Khajuraho, a very small town with only two small hotels. People travel there to see the temples and their carvings. The manager, who spoke English, loaned me a short-wave radio, and we managed to pick up some news about the rioting in different parts of the country.

The manager invited us to have a drink with him after dinner. When we joined him in the bar, he had already had a few drinks.

Suddenly the chef, who was more than six feet tall, came over to show the manager a telegram he had received. He seemed very upset.

"What's wrong?" I asked the manager.

"The message says that two hundred Hindus have arrived by train in New Delhi, murdered, with their heads cut off."

"Are you sure?" I asked. "Maybe this is a wild rumor. How do you know this is the truth?"

"We have a very reliable source," he said. "The chef and I are warriors. It is our duty once and for all to get rid of all Sikhs. They are troublemakers, and we just have to kill them."

A Sikh worked in the hotel. He was in his early twenties. The manager and the chef now planned to kill him out of a sense of duty.

Sandy and I overheard their plotting, and she went right up to the room. I could not believe what we had heard. I immediately began to tell the manager the story of my captivity and release. The three of us had some more drinks. As they became drunk, I invited them outside. I took them to the pool area where we talked for over two hours. I tried to reason with them.

"How long have you known him?" I asked.

"About three years," they said.

"Has he been a good worker?"

"Yes."

"Has he ever done any harm?"

"No."

"How can you kill him then? How can you take his life?" I asked. "Tomorrow you will not be able to live with yourself. Besides, just because you heard that two hundred Hindus got killed doesn't mean that it's true. Maybe there were only twenty, or two. By taking an innocent life, you would have to live for the rest of your life knowing that you committed cold-blooded murder."

After we had gone back and forth, the manager turned to the chef. He said, "Mr. Henry may have a very good point. Perhaps we should think it over." He then informed me that the Sikh would sleep in his room. "He will be safe," the manager said. I thanked him.

The next morning when I got up, the Sikh was behind his desk.

I never was able to learn the truth or untruth of the rumor, but at that moment I felt that no matter what else might happen in my life, my mission on earth was accomplished because I had saved a man's life.

WHAT WAS SO shocking to me in India was to realize how easy it was to influence ordinary people to kill their innocent neighbors. Within twenty-four hours of the assassination, Sikhs were being killed and their homes set on fire. It was also interesting that a minister of government, in this case the minister of tourism, was so quick to state that Pakistan was responsible, because of all the years of hate propaganda by India against Pakistan, Pakistan against India.

India is the largest country with a democratic system, but the country is very poor, and a government needs excuses for mismanagement. Therefore, they need an enemy, a scapegoat. To India, Pakistan seemed to be the enemy. Yes, I was very angry and disappointed at the way the Hindus behaved against their fellow man, but on the other hand, I found the majority of people in India to be kind, honest, and sensitive. I learned that there are more good people than bad in India, as I have found to be true also in other parts of the world to which I have traveled.

# Return
# to Russia

I N  D E C E M B E R  1 9 8 5 ,  I N  N E W  Y O R K ,  A N  E X H I B I -
tion was sponsored by the United Nations Center for Human Rights:
"Auschwitz — A Crime against Mankind." The exhibit was to remain
on display at the United Nations building for three months, till the end
of February 1986, and would then be available to travel for a period of
time in the United States. Upon my return home, I immediately started
working on bringing the Auschwitz exhibit to Seattle. I met again with
the Jewish Historical Society and gave them a report on what had tran-
spired in New York. I was willing to bring the exhibit to Seattle, provided
that I had their support. I was given the okay to look for a place and find
out how much it would cost. I visited the different museums in the area,
but I could not get any space on such short notice. I finally found space
at the Seattle Center, and the center agreed to co-sponsor the exhibit.
There would be no cost to us for the space.

I then had to work out a budget. I figured the cost would be a few
thousand dollars. I knew that I could raise that amount without difficulty.
I also got the Jewish Community Relations Council to come forward as
a supporting organization. I then reported back to the Jewish Historical

Society and asked them for their organizational support for the exhibit and their work to pull everything together. The president at that time, Joan Krivosha, was very helpful, and I secured the support of the executive committee by guaranteeing that there would be no cost to the society, even if I had to underwrite the exhibit personally.

Booth Gardner, then governor of our state, agreed to serve as my honorary co-chairman for this exhibit. This allowed me to include his name on the invitations to the opening ceremonies.

Jan Rabs, the Polish consul general, came to the opening, as did Maurice Goldstein, president of the International Auschwitz Committee in Belgium, and dignitaries from all over the state, including Seattle Mayor Charles Royer, several Seattle City Council members, congressmen, and senators.

In March 1987, during the three weeks of the exhibition in Seattle, over twenty-six thousand people attended. On the weekends there were very long lines waiting to come in. During the first week alone as many people attended as I had projected for the duration of the exhibit. There was standing room only, with people lined up outside waiting to get in. It was a great thrill for me to see this event come to our city, because I had been privileged to touch and help and work on every angle of bringing it here.

I remembered what Sandy had said to me after visiting the Mauthausen concentration camp. Perhaps there would never be another war if people could only see a Nazi concentration camp. Perhaps they would learn to live with and tolerate one another. I felt fulfilled in helping to bring to Seattle such a powerful exhibit of man's inhumanity to man.

I continued to enjoy life in America, but in the back of my mind I felt guilty about the people who had saved our lives in Ukraine. I continually wondered what had happened to them. When my father was alive, he discouraged me from contacting them. He was afraid to jeopardize their safety. Whenever I spoke to him, though, I tried to find out what had become of the family who saved us.

"Please," he told me, "leave those people in peace and let them live out their lives without being disturbed or endangered."

I had tried to visit Brody in the 1970s, but I couldn't get a visa. Now it was 1988. I knew that President Reagan was going to go to Russia sometime late in June. Relations between the two countries had improved. I felt it would be a good time for me to go to Russia. I began procedures to get my visa, airplane tickets, and hotel reservations. This took some time to accomplish, but we finally had our plans set.

We had to list all the jewelry we brought in to Russia, and it took us over an hour to get through customs. First, they couldn't measure Sandy's diamond ring. They did not believe that these were real diamonds, so they sent for a special jeweler to come in. An official looked at my passport and wanted to know if I had any relatives. I said no. I didn't tell him that they had all been killed.

After we finally got through customs, we drove to the In-Tourist Hotel on Gorky Street, overlooking the Kremlin. From our room we could see the Kremlin walls and the center of Red Square. We had a suite consisting of a reception room and a separate bedroom, but the furniture was old.

I decided to wear my Star of David in Russia. I felt that I had suffered enough for being a Jew, and I was not going to be ashamed. I wanted them to know that I was back after all these years and was proud of my Jewishness.

Forty-three years had passed since I had left Eastern Europe. I had wondered many times what would have happened to me if I had stayed. How successful would I have become? Being in Moscow, I realized how fortunate I was to live in the United States of America. I woke up at 3:30 a.m. thinking about my father. I wished that he were alive, so that when I got back from this trip, I could tell him how smart he had been and how thankful I felt.

In the morning we walked by ourselves near the Kremlin walls. Then we went on a tour and saw the changing of the guards at Lenin's tomb. I was surprised to hear the guide criticize Stalin. We had passed a building that was built in the Stalinist era. The building looked like a tractor. The guide told that us most of the elite people and close friends of Stalin had lived in this building in the 1930s, but that Stalin had them all killed.

On Saturday we decided to visit the one and only large synagogue in Moscow. This was the first time, since before World War II, that I heard a cantor with an additional six or eight men chanting. Tears came to my eyes as I listened to those haunting melodies. I had a conversation with a seventy-eight-year-old gentleman. Most of the people inside the synagogue were old, or at least over fifty. The rabbi, however, looked like a young person, perhaps in his forties. And the president of the synagogue looked to be in his late forties.

A young man had approached me outside the synagogue and asked if I would sell him the embroidered yarmulke I was wearing. "No," I said. "You can have it after I've gone inside and finished praying." I gave it to him after the service. He did not want to accept a gift, so he handed me ten rubles, then worth about twenty dollars. Another young man joined us and persuaded us to stay and talk with him, instead of taking a cab directly back to the hotel. He was nineteen years old. He had applied to go to Israel and he had an opportunity to go there via Bucharest, but he did not want to go that way because then he would *definitely* have to go to Israel. Instead, he wanted to go to Vienna so he would have time to decide whether to go to Israel or to the United States. He was a pacifist. When he was drafted into the Russian army, he was put away for three months because he refused to serve or to fire a weapon. His father was a communist who did not want to leave Russia, and his parents had provided very little Jewish upbringing. His grandfather, he claimed, was a rabbi.

It was very interesting to talk to this young man. He was proud to be Jewish, but he did not know if there was a God or if there wasn't. He didn't know how to read or understand Hebrew. He felt Jewish, but he had a difficult time explaining why. He clearly remembered one experience, though, which bonded us together. On his papers it said that he was a Jew, and that he had been kicked out of the university because of that.

LATER IN THE WEEK we visited two synagogues in Leningrad (St. Petersburg), a large one that was ninety-five years old, and a smaller one just over a hundred years old. The two synagogues made up one huge building and were very interesting. The large synagogue was closed, but the smaller one was open and people were inside saying prayers. The synagogues stood within a gated courtyard, and the wrought iron gates bore the Star of David. We were introduced to the vice president of the synagogue and he showed us around the large synagogue. I asked him what American Jews could do to help out.

"Send money," he said. "We have enough prayer shawls and tefillin. We have enough books now, but money would help because the building needs repairs."

There were about fifteen older gentlemen praying in the synagogue that morning. I learned that on the High Holy Days nearly five thousand people come to that synagogue. I also learned that many of the young people had left for Israel. Many Jews were over sixty and lived on a pension. The vice president of the synagogue in Leningrad told me that he did not want to go to Israel or America. He was settled there. His relatives were there. He knew his pension would come in, no matter what.

He introduced me to another gentleman, also a vice president of the synagogue, whose son and daughter-in-law had left for America. They were both engineers but were having a very difficult time making it in the United States.

# *Reunion*

ALL THE TIME THAT I WAS IN MOSCOW AND Leningrad during that spring visit in 1988, I had been looking forward to my return to Brody. Finally, the day came. We boarded an Aeroflot flight from Leningrad and flew to Lvov, where an Aeroflot representative met us and took us to a waiting car. The woman spoke German, and when I showed her my itinerary, she said: "Impossible. Your destination is for Lvov only, and therefore you cannot go to Brody."

I became very upset.

"I came all this way just so I could go to Brody," I said.

"It's Friday evening," she said. "On the weekend, nobody's working. If it were a Monday we could make some arrangements. But on weekends it is impossible."

"I don't care," I said. "You must do something. You must find me a way out of here. If you don't, I will go to Brody anyway, on my own."

"Oh no, please don't, because you will be arrested."

She made a phone call.

"Okay," she said. " A representative of the government will come to interview you at eleven o'clock tomorrow morning."

We were driven to a hotel overlooking the city of Lvov. We had not eaten any dinner, and it was nearly midnight. We also had a visit from Rosa Zacharow and her son, Sasha. Rosa is the sister of my aunt Nina, who is married to my uncle Salomon in Israel. Rosa and Sasha wanted Sandy and me to spend the next evening with them, but I told them that we would be going, no matter what, to Brody. Sasha offered to drive us to Brody the next day.

THE NEXT MORNING we all had breakfast together. When I went to the desk to see what was happening, I was told there was a gentleman waiting to speak to me. This was Ivan Kowal, director of internal security in Lvov, who had come to interview me. Mr. Kowal was very polite, and we spoke for maybe forty-five minutes. He wanted to know why the Jews had left Russia. He gave us permission to go to Brody and Suchowola, provided that we use an official car. I remember clearly the last thing he told me: "Please do not get mad at me," he said. "I'm going to try and give you good advice, not as a representative of the government, but because I like you. Take off the Star of David that you are wearing. The people of Brody and Suchowola still don't like Jews. If you want to get some help when you get into the region, remove your necklace. They are very anti-Semitic." Sandy agreed with him, so I wore a necktie, and it covered up my Star of David when we went to the Brody area that afternoon.

I first wanted to go to Suchowola, where our family property was, where we were in hiding. When we reached the village, I couldn't believe what I saw. It was not the same Suchowola that I had left. The bridge was really not as long as I had visualized. The river that used to run next to our property was almost dry, and it was only May.

Even before coming into Suchowola, I had noticed certain changes. Most of the peasants' houses used to be covered with straw. Now all the homes had metal or tile roofs. We drove to where our property had been. I knew where the place was that we hid — but somehow everything had gotten moved around. The houses were changed, and I was in a panic. I was frightened because I had a map in my head, but the way the village looked now had been changed by the war and time. I told Sasha, who was driving us, to ask a person approaching if he knew about the Friedmans, and if he had lived in Suchowola before World War II.

This man hadn't heard of our family, but he suggested that we go to the home of Ilja Kupchinski, the oldest resident in the village. So we did. Mr. Kupchinski was probably in his nineties, and he said, "Oh, yes, yes, yes. I remember Jacob Friedman and his wife. Oh Dora, I remember her!" He called me "Heniek" (my nickname as a child) and said, "You got your mother's hair, her curly hair—what a lady she was!"

He went on and on. He was full of praise about my father. When his horse died, my father had loaned him two horses to finish his harvesting. He now came with us and pointed out where our property had been. I was incredulous. Our house was gone. There was not a building standing. The grounds were covered in tall grass as if nothing had ever been there, yet in a flash I remembered the house, the barns, the fun times my family and I had had on this land. When I looked at that silent meadow of grass, I felt cramps in my stomach.

Then we went to the neighbor's place where my father had hidden and Isaac had joined him. Even that building, that barn, was changed, rebuilt with a different roof. The farmer no longer had a horse, but he did have a cow and a calf and pigs. I took pictures. I also met the niece of the woman who had hidden my father and Isaac and, for one week, my entire family, including Sarah. That woman, Mrs. Bazalchik, and her husband had died of natural causes, but her two sons were killed under mysterious circumstances that nobody wanted to talk about.

As we were walking with Mr. Kupchinski, I spotted a man on crutches with one leg. I recognized him as a schoolmate with whom I'd played before the Nazis came. I remembered how he lost his leg. During the war, we kids used to take the fuse out from unexploded shells and then light a match to the inside of the powder, shooting great flames into the air. Somehow, when he was trying to take the fuse out, the shell exploded and blew his leg off. Now here he was, leaning on a crutch and digging a ditch near his house with two buddies helping him. We talked for a while.

I was afraid to expose the people who had hidden us during the war, so I asked questions very carefully. But then I blurted out and asked whether the Symchucks were still alive. I desperately wanted to know what had happened to them. As I was saying this, someone said: "Oh, there goes Julia." She was leading her cow to pasture, and I started yelling: "Hold, hold, hold!" Meanwhile, one of the gentlemen joined our conversation at the ditch, and he wanted to know who the people were who had helped us survive.

"I'm not at liberty to tell you who those people were," I said. "If they wanted you to know that they had hidden Jews, they would have told you themselves."

"Well," he said, "it's no difference to me now, but it would be interesting to know."

That ended the conversation, because I was desperate to meet up with Julia Symchuck, the daughter of the couple who hid us. I ran up to her.

"It's me, Heniek!" I said.

"Who?" She look confused.

"Dora's son!" I shouted.

Suddenly she realized who I was. She became very excited. Her cow almost got hit by a car because she wasn't looking.

Julia was responsible for my being alive today. As I never tire of saying, when she was eighteen and working for the police department as a cleaning maid, she overheard a conversation at the station and then warned my father to run before the Gestapo came to take him away.

Her mother Mary, the angel who took care of us up in the attic, was seventy years old when she died in 1973. Julia took us to meet her father Ivan, who was then over ninety years old. He was not so vigorous as Mr. Kupchinski and did not know who I was. He died a few months later at the age of ninety-three. We met Julia's niece and her two grandnieces, who lived with her. I was very excited and very emotional. Julia took out a bottle of champagne to celebrate. We exchanged small gifts, and I promised I would do more for her in the future. I took down her address and promised to contact her. Before I got back in the car, we embraced.

Our reunion was brief, as I wanted to see Brody before dark. I had permission to be in that area only for a day. It was explained to me that Brody was off limits to tourists because it was the site of an important military installation. I don't know if that was true, but it was the reason given to me. We arrived in Brody just as the sun was setting, and by accident, we came to the old part of town where the ghetto used to be. The Great Synagogue was collapsing. The walls, however, were still standing.

New high-rise apartments were built around the synagogue. It was a sorry sight, and it reminded me of all the Jews who perished in Brody.

As I was filming and taking pictures, a gentleman walked by and he said, "I am Russian. I came to live in Brody in 1945."

"Do you know any Jews?" I asked.

"No," he said. "Since 1945 I've run into only three Jews."

"At one time in Brody and the surrounding area there were fifteen thousand Jews," I said. While I went on to take some more pictures, he walked over to talk quietly with Sasha, who, as our driver, had stayed with the car.

As we left Brody and were on our way back to Lvov, Sasha told me what the man had said to him. He apparently thought Sasha was the KGB watching me, and he told him, "Any kike that's left should be hung by his neck. Watch this guy, because you can't trust a kike."

I was very upset with Sasha for not telling me what the man was saying while he was saying it, or calling me into this conversation, because I probably would have broken my camera on the man's head. My heart was crying for my relatives and all the Jews who had perished, and this son of a bitch could make a statement like that. I must say, though, that the people that I spoke with in Suchowola who had known our family seemed very friendly and happy to see us. And I knew that our visit would be the topic of conversation for some time to come.

In Brody, I was very disappointed because most of the older buildings had been torn down. I could not find anything recognizable. I could not find my way to the house where we had once lived; I could not find where we had stayed from 1944 to 1945. Everything was turned around. Streets were changed. It was a new city. I left, my heart bleeding. But in a way, after seeing those people, the way they still live, I felt very fortunate to have gone to America. During times like that, I would ask myself: "How could I be a normal person after all the things that I lived through?"

The next day I asked to see Ivan Kowal, the government official who had originally given me permission to travel to Brody. I wanted to inform him about the situation there. He agreed to meet me at three o'clock on Sunday afternoon, even though his mother was having a birthday celebration at that time. I appreciated the effort he was making for me.

When we returned from touring the city, he was waiting for me in the lobby of my hotel. We went up to my room and had a drink of scotch.

Then I explained to him my concerns about the synagogue in Brody, standing the way it was without any acknowledgment of history or the Jews who died in Brody. I also mentioned the synagogue in Lvov, which was locked up, unsafe to enter, and nearly in ruins. I was wondering if something could be done, perhaps to raise money.

"Commemorative plaques at those sites are impossible at this time," he said. "The synagogue in Brody still stands because the government does not have the money to destroy the building. In other words, the government has to spend its money on new housing and roads. We realize the benefits, perhaps, that there could be in making these relics into museums. They will be historically of value to future generations. But at this point, we can not accept money from the United States or Israel. It would not look right if the government did anything to restore Jewish synagogues."

"But that's an outrage," I said.

"I will promise you one thing," he said. "I will send you archival documents of the massacre of Jews, documentary evidence of the crimes that were committed by certain people who are living right now in America and in Canada, free from prosecution."

I learned that he himself had done research in connection with Nazi war criminals. He told me that written records exist to this day of the atrocities perpetrated on the Jews. This was because the Ukrainian police and other Nazi officials were required to write down the exact names of the people who were killed, along with the names of those who had escaped.

OUR TRIP WAS winding down, but before returning home we had the pleasure of having dinner with my aunt Nina's sister, Rosa, and her family in Lvov. Rosa Zacharow and her husband Michael were Jewish. Their two sons, Sasha and Wladimar, were married to non-Jewish women but were listed as Jewish on their Soviet passports. Their three grandchildren lived with them as well. They served us a sumptuous feast. Rosa told us that none of the food was available in the government stores where she shops. It was all bought on the outside market. Their home consisted of three rooms, including a study room shared by their two sons and daughters-in-law. They owned a very small television. The kitchen was so tiny, I don't know how they all managed in it. Nine people lived in this crowded apartment, yet they felt very fortunate to have what they did. The husband belonged to the Communist Party, and he wouldn't have his picture taken for fear of being exposed. He was afraid to be associated with a foreigner. Obviously, he knew the psychology of the system. But it was upsetting to me to see how people were still afraid, how they had to pull the plug on the telephone for fear somebody was listening in.

Nevertheless, they were a happy family. The elder statesman of the house had no intention of leaving Russia. He was a loyal communist and wouldn't even discuss politics with me.

We also visited a Jewish cemetery, and I was surprised at how well kept it was, and at how many people were visiting it and bringing flowers. We found one old couple who spoke Yiddish, and they explained to me that many of the Jewish people now intermarry with Gentiles. They come and visit their loved ones there. It was Shavuoth, the day that celebrates the giving of the Ten Commandments to Moses. And it was surprising to me to see so many people aware of the holiday, even though they had very little Jewish education. Even Rosa's husband Michael, the committed communist, celebrated Passover. They got their matzoth from Leningrad or Moscow.

According to one source, 1.8 percent of the Ukrainian population is Jewish, but nobody knows how many Jews live in Lvov. The three synagogues were locked after the 1967 Arab–Israel War, because Russia broke off diplomatic relations with Israel and this was a way to punish the Jews.

I wished that I could have spent more time in Brody and Suchowola. We had only one day. I would have liked more time, because I don't think I will ever pass that way again.

I did accomplish my mission, though. I found the Symchuck family. I promised myself to bring Julia Symchuck to America for a visit, and I intended to start working on this project as soon as I got home.

# A Heroine
# in Seattle

S ANDY AND I STARTED WORKING TO BRING
Julia Symchuck to Seattle for a visit with our family. Since my return from Russia, I had sent her packages; I also sent her money
to buy an airline ticket.

I was working with an official in Russia to help her with her passport, airplane ticket, and other details. In March 1989 Julia wrote to tell
me that the only time she could get a ticket out of Russia was in April of
1990. That seemed like a long time to wait. I wrote to Ivan Kowal, the director of internal security in Lvov whom I had befriended on my 1988
visit and who had sent me material from the Lvov archives, to see if he
could expedite Julia's coming to America.

In the meantime, I had been asked to chair the Passage to Freedom
campaign in Seattle, working with other organizations nationwide to
raise 35 million dollars to help Soviet Jews escape oppression and go
wherever they wished to live. I could still remember the people who had
helped me come to this great country, and I felt absolutely obligated
to help however I could. We committed ourselves to raise $465,000 in
the greater Seattle area. Many people told me this was an unreachable

figure. But to me, it was a challenge. I was fortunate to get the support of the community and especially the full support of the local rabbis. I made arrangements to leave for Italy after July, to study the conditions under which Russian Jews had to live while waiting for emigration to the United States.

While I was involved with organizing fund-raising for the Russian Jews, I got a telegram on July 10 from Julia stating that she was arriving on July 13 in Washington, D.C., only three days hence! My friend Ivan Kowal had secured space for her on a diplomatic flight from Moscow, on the Russian Aeroflot airline. It was fortunate that our nephew worked in Washington, D.C., because I assumed that Julia didn't realize how far that city was from here, and therefore she probably had not ordered a ticket from Washington to Seattle. I remembered all those years ago, in Austria, when I received my papers to go to Seattle, Washington. I believed that I was going to the capital of the U.S.A. to live, and that is exactly what Julia believed — that Seattle was in Washington, D.C., and not three thousand miles away in Washington state.

I made arrangements immediately, without knowing all the details, to express-mail round-trip airplane tickets for Julia to my nephew. I asked him to meet her when she arrived on the Aeroflot flight, and to put her on a plane to Seattle. I was correct in my assumption that she did not have a ticket from Washington, D.C., to Seattle. This was her first time on a plane and the first time she had ever been to a different country, so how would she know the logistics?

But I was surprised that people did not inform her of the fact that Washington, D.C., was a long way from Seattle. Julia was very fortunate the telegram reached me before I had left for Europe. I still shiver when I think of what might have happened had she arrived in Washington, D.C., and I had been in Rome.

Julia arrived in Seattle on July 13, 1989, and my family, including all my grandchildren, were there to meet her. It was wonderful to greet her after so many years. I had arranged for television and newspaper coverage of her arrival at the airport. Julia gave a press interview, and then we took her home.

She had a suitcase with her, but the suitcase contained only a bottle of Russian vodka and a bottle of champagne, no clothes. For the time being, my wife gave Julia some of her own clothes to wear, including a nightgown. We found out that Julia had spent three days in Moscow sleeping on benches in the street because there were no accommodations available for her. She could not go into a restaurant and eat while in Moscow, so she ate the small amount of food that she brought with her.

The next day we bought her new clothes and shoes. When we were out shopping, she took off her shoes. Her feet were bleeding. She had worn the same dress and the same pair of shoes for five days. It almost made me sick. Sandy and Julia were very congenial. They somehow understood each other, even though they could not really communicate properly in two different languages.

After Julia had clothes and other necessities, the next thing to do was make arrangements to get her teeth fixed. Every day during her first three weeks in America, we went to the dentist, because she had so much work to be done in her mouth. This particular dentist had read Julia's story from my interview in the Bellevue *Journal American* after my trip to the Soviet Union. He called me and said that if Julia ever came to visit me, he would be happy to do the work for only the price of materials. It's wonderful that there are such good people everywhere, understanding people.

The dentist and I were surprised at how Julia was able to live with so many rotten teeth in her mouth. So I asked her if she had any pain. "Oh, yes," she said. "I have pain, but I get used to it and I don't pay attention to it anymore."

We also felt that Julia should have a facial, a massage, and a new hairdo—the whole works. After all this, she looked like an entirely different person. She was becoming quite well known in the Seattle community. Two local newspapers carried photographs of her, and the local television channels ran features on her.

Julia also received an award from Governor Booth Gardner. She was recognized in congress by Rod Chandler, and she received a certificate from the King County Council. In addition, beyond our shores, she was honored by Israel with their highest civilian award, the medal of the Righteous Gentile among Nations. The Israeli consul general, Harry Kney-Tal, flew here from San Francisco to grant this award. Julia had her picture taken with the Israeli ambassador, who was on a visit to Seattle.

I took Julia to a dairy farm, and we also visited the Space Needle in Seattle, which was the highest place she had ever been. There were parties in her honor. We also held a news conference at my home. The story she told disturbed and upset me, because it brought back all the bad memories. When asked whether she would tell other people in her village about what her family did for mine in saving our lives, she responded: "What good will that do? I don't think so. I don't care about my safety, but I feel that they may harm my niece and my grandniece, as well as my nephew and his family."

About two weeks later she was interviewed again, this time for a television station. She had changed her mind about what she would say upon returning to Suchowola. After her visit with us, she felt that she should go back and tell what her family had done for us. I did not have to encourage her to make those statements; she decided on her own.

I thought of my father, who did not want to jeopardize the safety of the Symchuck family by exposing them. I had to give him credit for his wisdom, even though for many years I had thought he was wrong for not trying to find and help them. Unfortunately, Julia was the only one left in the family, because her parents and brothers and sister were dead. Now she felt determined to share the truth, no matter what the consequences.

It was wonderful to behold Julia's expression of appreciation at the things she was able to see and do in Seattle. There were so many firsts for her. She was sixty-five now and she felt it had been worthwhile going through all the hardships, just to come here and see the wonders she had not seen before. We took her on a boat to the Olympic Peninsula. She now worships the ocean. In her country, the only boating possible is on a river. There are no lakes or oceans. The Olympic Mountains were amazing to her.

When I took her to the airport, she said that she had arrived in the evening and now she was leaving in the evening. She said that the time she had spent with us felt like a dream. She had a difficult time believing that this had really happened to her. She had been honored in so many ways, though in her own country she had never been honored with anything except hard work. For me, in a way, it was like a burden lifted from my shoulders, to do something nice for a person who deserved it so much. It was a responsibility and perhaps an obligation that I felt up till then I had not fulfilled.

I planned to help her and her family after her return to Russia. And as much as Julia enjoyed her stay with us, I equally enjoyed the ability to entertain her. I enjoyed it more than anything else in life that I'd done before.

I FEEL VERY GOOD that I was able to help Julia Symchuck and her family in Russia with material things. I later received a letter from her. She had been invited by the Ukraine to come to the fiftieth anniversary of the commemoration of the massacre of Jews in Babi Yar. I am sure Julia never would have been recognized or even invited if she had remained silent upon her return to her country. No. She shared her story on national television, and because of her conviction she was invited to participate in this fifty-year commemoration. She was honored for her humane achievement, for risking her life in order to save other human beings.

# Hope

THERE WAS A TIME IN MY LIFE AFTER THE war when I felt ashamed that I was a Jew because of what had happened to us as a people. I felt guilty because I had survived and most of my relatives had not. Why was I alive, and why were they dead? It took me a while to realize how fortunate I am to be a Jew. The Jewish seeds were planted in me when I was a child growing up, and I turned out to be who I am because of these Jewish values.

In 1990 the Seattle Jewish community named me "Volunteer of the Year." I was honored by the many people who attended the award dinner and generously gave me a standing ovation. Also in 1990, along with many other Holocaust survivors, as well as senators and other dignitaries, I took part in the Washington, D.C., conference initiating the campaign to raise funds for a national Holocaust museum.

Recently my wife asked me a question in casual conversation: If I had a chance to be in someone else's shoes, whose shoes would I pick? I gave this question a lot of thought, and my answer was that I would not choose to step into the shoes of any of my friends or acquaintances, because I am very content and happy with who I am. I do feel, however, that

I have missed out by not being better educated. I feel out of place at times because of a lack of knowledge. Oh, I am street smart. I educated myself on many different subjects, but I wish I had a better academic background.

By doing this, however, by finishing this book, I believe that I have at last fulfilled what my youngest son, Jeffrey, wanted me to do so many years ago.

Library of Congress Cataloging-in-Publication Data
Friedman, Henry
I'm no hero : journeys of a Holocaust survivor / Henry Friedman;
foreword by Michael Berenbaum.
p.    cm.
"A Samuel & Althea Stroum book."
ISBN 0-295-97801-5 (cloth)
1. Friedman, Henry.    2. Jews—Persecutions—Ukraine—Brody.
3. Holocaust, Jewish (1939–1945)—Ukraine—Brody Personal narratives.
4. Brody (Ukraine) Biography.    5. Righteous Gentiles in the
Holocaust—Ukraine—Brody.    6. Jewish children in the Holocaust—
Ukraine—Brody Biography.    7. Holocaust survivors—Washington
(State)—Seattle Biography.    8. Seattle (Wash.) Biography.    I. Title.
DS135.U43F754    1999
940.53'18'092—dc21    99-29844
CIP